The Path Less Traveled

Living with Divine Intention in a Secular World

Debbie Caudle

Copyright © 2020 by **Debbie Caudle**

All rights reserved. No part of this publication may be reproduced, distributed, or transmitted in any form or by any means, without prior written permission.

All Scripture quotations are taken from the Holy Bible, New King James translation ®. Used by permission. All rights reserved worldwide.

*All names are changed to protect privacy

Speak It To Book
www.speakittobook.com

The Path Less Traveled / Debbie Caudle
ISBN-13: 978-1-952602-20-7

This book is dedicated to those who have loved me, despite all my shortcomings; who have supported and encouraged me through so many ups and downs, held my hand, wiped my tears away and never stopped believing, even when I wanted to. You know who you are. Thank you.

CONTENTS

Nothing Ventured, Nothing Gained 3
The Two Paths 10
The Intentional Way 24
Intentionality and Intimacy 39
What's the Point? 57
Time to Dream 73
The Pyramid Perspective 95
A Sidetracked Dream 115
Turning Dreams into Reality 127
Oops! You've Lost Your Way 145
Intentionality in Motion 172
Forgiveness 193
Seeking an Abundant Life 205
Notes 207
About the Author 209
About Speak It To Book 210

INTRODUCTION

Nothing Ventured, Nothing Gained

It comes seemingly from nowhere. It is sudden, and it is scary. I start to breathe quickly, and I am bombarded with anxious thoughts swirling around in my head like a kaleidoscope. Something is sitting on my chest, weighing me down. My heart is racing, and my eyes fill with tears. I squeeze my nails into my palms to distract myself as I look around. Does anyone notice? Why is this happening? All I can do in this moment is pray.

It's called a panic attack, and I experienced my first one in the summer of 2013. They would come out of nowhere. Sometimes I'd be with my friends. I'd be sitting in the back of a car, trying to listen to the conversation while fighting back complete panic. What had provoked it? Did one of my friends trigger it with something she said?

Other times I'd lie in bed at night and feel like a giant elephant was on top of me, making it hard to breathe. I'd get in my car to drive somewhere and find myself overwhelmed with tears.

Even so, mine weren't horrible, as panic attacks go. As

a therapist, I'd heard panic attacks described by clients in various ways over the years. Thankfully I only experienced them for a few months, and then God mercifully removed them from me. After experiencing panic attacks firsthand, I wouldn't wish them on anyone.

My panic attacks were the culmination of a lot of things. For too long I'd been living on autopilot, worrying about countless "what ifs" that I was trying to solve on my own. I'd taken on things that weren't my sole responsibility, and the burden of that self-inflicted load was heavy.

I knew it. I knew what it was doing to me. I just didn't see a way out.

It was like a dark cloud hovering over me, following me wherever I went—even though the sun seemed to shine brightly on everyone else. Even the simplest tasks felt burdensome. My mind was in a fog, and if I thought too far ahead, panic would send me into a tailspin.

I was trying to control too many things instead of letting God handle them for me. I was *afraid* to let go. I was afraid to trust that somehow, *some way*, God would work things out for the best.

I thought I had to do it all, and it was exhausting. It drained me in every possible way. It affected my physical health, my mental wellbeing, and my ability to give to others professionally. It was not sustainable.

Then, finally, I acknowledged that I was, after all, *human*. I needed help. No matter what the consequences—failure, loss of income, loss of home, loss of health—it was time to make some serious changes. It was time for a different path—a path that focused on living with full, God-directed intention. I had to see it though. I had to recognize the crossroads in front of me. I had to take complete responsibility for the choice to take a new path, and I had to have the courage to walk it.

I see you too. I see you walking your own path, but maybe it's not the path you would have chosen all those years ago. Perhaps it's the path of least resistance. It's familiar, you know it well.

Maybe you've shut down, pretending you don't care anymore. You've switched to autopilot, just going through the daily motions of living.

If so, is it because that seems easier?

I know that feeling. I know how exhausting it can be to even *think* about living intentionally. It's easier to ignore it. Fill that void with other things. Those things, while satisfying in the moment, leave you empty and craving more.

It's scary to think about change. It's scary to think about the *consequences* of changing. It's scary to think about the *work* and *time* it takes to change.

It does take work. It takes hard work. It's worth it though, I can attest to that. My journey isn't over, just as yours isn't. I have lots of changing ahead of me, but what I've learned so far is worth sharing.

I'm getting ahead of myself, though.

I'm a therapist and coach. I've worked with women of all ages for over twenty-six years—women who share common struggles and challenges, despite their different backgrounds. I'm also a Christian woman who has experienced many of those same struggles—and tried to find meaning and purpose in those struggles with God's help. As you read further, you will discover I come from both a professional *and* personal perspective in writing this book.

I *know* how hard life can be. I *know* you have dealt with some unexpected (and painful) things already. And you've made choices in response to those experiences.

A Call to Action

Every woman comes to a point in life when she reaches a crossroads—a point where a decision has to be made. *You* will come to a point where a decision has to be made. Maybe you are there right now.

You can continue down the life path of familiarity, the one strewn with disappointment, hurt, trauma, and betrayal. The path where people have let you down, and you've let yourself down. Where expectations are unmet, and poor choices lead to consequences. This path isn't healthy or productive, but it is well-traveled (which makes it seemingly *easier* to continue on this path).

You can also choose a different life path—the one less traveled. This path moves you away from the debris and obstacles that burden you. It moves you toward your intentions and goals. This new path leads to understanding God's purpose for you. It leads to greater peace and contentment.

There's just one small problem: the path less traveled has a bend in it that you can't see around. *You don't know what lies ahead,* and that's scary.

Yes, change is scary. Intentional living, though, requires a willingness to change. That's why this new path is less traveled. We may talk about wanting to change, but how many of us actually do the hard work to make it happen? Change requires a willingness to take a long, hard look at the path we're on as women and why. Are we on the familiar path, yet feeling miserable? Are we blaming circumstances, our childhood, our spouse, ourselves, or even missed opportunities? Are we feeling angry, resentful, and bitter? Do we feel powerless to change our situation so instead we just gripe and complain about the unfairness of it all?

That's certainly one option, but it's not the one I want to choose. Not anymore. You see, I know a thing or two about the familiar path, just like you. I know it from experience, professionally and personally. I've counseled and coached hundreds of women over the years and watched them choose the familiar path over and over again. I've heard all the excuses and made them myself.

I know.

Yes, I know it's hard.

This book is a call to action. It's a call to all women who, like me, are in search of more—more confidence, more clarity, more abundance, and more peace of mind. And not just for themselves but for their loved ones as well. Because *those* women know that the only way they can achieve that is if they start making different choices. Intentional choices. *Those* women know that the only path to real, sustainable happiness is through their relationship with God. That only He can give them the confidence to know that they have worth; that they are deeply precious to Him. Only He can give them the clarity to understand the hurts of the past. And the ability to leave them there. Only He can give us the ability to *see* abundance in our lives, even in the midst of challenges. Only through following Him will we find our way to true peace of mind.

Are you one of *those* women? Are you at a crossroads in your life? Are you contemplating making changes but scared about the consequences? It's true that anytime you set out to make intentional changes in your life you will set in motion a series of unforeseen events. There's no way to completely predict the responses of others. Some will applaud you. Some will doubt your motives. Some may be disapproving or unsupportive.

Does that mean that you shouldn't change?

This book is not meant to empower women to set aside their responsibilities, obligations, and commitments. I am not advocating abandoning your marriage, your family, or your church in pursuit of self-fulfillment. Rather, this book is about *taking responsibility* for the one person you can manage—yourself. It's about recognizing that if life isn't what you want it to be, it's partly your fault, and only you can do something about it.

What do you want?

That's a question I want you to spend a lot of time thinking about while you read this book. And here's another one.

What does God want of you?

If what you want doesn't mesh with God's plan for you, then it won't matter how hard you work to change. Your efforts will be wasted. God *intends* for you to be intentional. He *desires* for you to have abundance. He *wants* you to seek Him out for direction and He is willing to guide you.

So choose your path wisely, but do choose. You don't get where you want to go by not making decisions, or by abdicating your responsibilities to others. Don't be pulled along by others or circumstances. Yes, time and chance happen to us all. Yes, we all experience the effects of others' choices in our lives at times. Yes, some things do happen that we can't control, for reasons that seem incomprehensible at the time, and yes, not all our efforts to be intentional work out the way we want or in the timeframe we want.

We must still choose. If nothing else, we can choose our attitude. We can choose to change our perspective. We can choose to learn from the things we experience, from the situations and circumstances we can't control. We can choose to trust that God is truly in charge of all things, at all times.

If you're that woman—a woman who's ready to make the tough choices, to be accountable for herself and accountable to God—then I welcome you on this journey with me. I congratulate you for taking the first step toward that new, unfamiliar path—the path less traveled.

CHAPTER ONE

The Two Paths

Remember when you were young, and you had your whole life ahead of you just waiting to be lived? You had dreams, and you were filled with anticipation and passion about accomplishing them?

How did you get from that place to where you are now?

Imagine that you're walking down a path. It's a fairly wide path, and others are traveling it with you. You can look back over your shoulder and see where you've been, and you can look ahead and predict—with some accuracy—where you're going. That's because this path is *familiar;* it's what you know. It's not an easy path, nor is it always comfortable. In fact, the choices that keep you on this path are often hurtful and damaging.

The Familiar Path

The familiar path is the path of least resistance. If that's the path you're traveling right now, it took time to get that way. It didn't happen overnight, and you're on it for three reasons: the choices you've made, the choices you've *not* made, and the choices that others have made for you. Those choices—some good, some bad—have had consequences.

One consequence, perhaps, is that you gave up on your dreams somewhere along the way. You stopped believing they could be achieved.

Perhaps you've made it your life's mission to take care of other people and help them reach their potential, while your own is left unnurtured. Perhaps it feels selfish to look after yourself while others need something from you.

One of the problems with staying on the path you're on is that you *didn't choose it*—not consciously that is. No one ever intends to choose a path that is littered with the fallout of bad choices, the anguish caused by disappointments, unmet expectations, hurt, and trauma.

However, we humans are prone to self sabotage. We practice poor decision-making until we turn it into an art form. We become plagued with doubt, insecurities, limiting beliefs, faulty thinking, and bad habits. Over time we begin to question our ability to choose a different way. We become victims of circumstance, powerless to do anything but be tugged along. We don't learn from the past; we wallow in it.

Then fear sets in, stealing our confidence and our belief that we can change.

Have you become complacent? Not comfortable, just—settled? Life may not be great on your current path, but it's good enough, right? If that's what you're telling yourself, you may be in denial.

Denial is tricky. Short-term denial can help in the moment. It can give you time to adjust to new circumstances, or the uncertainty of them. However, it becomes harmful when it gets in the way of you taking decisive action to change your circumstances. Telling yourself that you don't need to be happy, that happiness can't be achieved in this lifetime, that it's too late to change, that you don't deserve it, or don't know how, are all just excuses you (and I) use to stay stuck.

We may also default to the familiar (though ever so painful), because too many of us approach middle age still clinging to the idea that our needs and desires ought to be fulfilled by others. We find ourselves unhappy and unsatisfied, so we blame others. We try to find fulfillment in temporary things.

The problem is, no matter who we blame, and no matter how much we chase after self-fulfillment, it's never enough. Sex, romance, shopping, food, alcohol, exercise, money, recognition, power—none of these bring about lasting happiness.

A Crisis of Truth

Then we come to the crossroads I've been talking about. It's a place where our current path diverges, and another path appears in the distance. We face a choice. "Do I stay where I am, or do I move to this other path?"

Sometimes that choice is made for us because of circumstances. Events are set in motion that force us to take a long, hard look at where we are versus where we want to be. Other times the choice is internal. We *wake up* and realize we're headed somewhere we don't want to go and only we can do something about it.

For a lot of women this happens between their mid-thirties and forties, though not always. Sometimes it can happen to us when we're much younger. It's not always one event that brings us to that crisis of truth. It can be a series of occurrences, or re-occurrences because if you're stubborn like me, you might need several wake- up calls.

How can you know that it's time to switch paths?
There are clear signs:

- Discontent with yourself
- Discontent with your marriage

- Anger and resentment towards people and situations
- Chronic feelings of overwhelm, stress, anxiety and/or depression
- Chronic irritability over the "little" things
- Stress-induced illnesses
- Feelings of victimization
- Bitterness
- Feelings of powerlessness or hopelessness
- Wanting (or feeling obligated) to control everything (and everyone)

When you come to that realization, a new path emerges. The other path was always there, of course. It's just not well traveled. That's because it's the harder path, at least initially. It's narrower, steeper, and you will face resistance if you choose it.

You will also set things in motion—for yourself *and* others—that you can't fully anticipate or control.

That means there's a bend in this path that you can't see around, which makes it all the harder to take, so some stay on the familiar path because at least it's, well—familiar!

The other path is the path of intentionality. It's the path of personal accountability. It's the path of taking responsibility for the discontent you're experiencing, and it's determining to change what is in your power to change from this point forward. It's the path that leads you to true fulfillment because the real problem is—if you've been traveling the familiar path—you've been looking for fulfillment in the wrong place.

Crossing the Bridge

We live in a time when many don't believe in God while others say they do. In reality though, He has no day-to-day involvement in their lives.

What about you? Is God relevant to you? What does that even mean?

As women, we are bombarded with messages that tell us to pursue our own happiness, and that self-fulfillment is the most significant thing in life. These messages are everywhere: in magazines, on billboards, in song lyrics, and on the pages of books. Television shows and movies constantly portray an ideal for women that says we should be strong and self-reliant. We just need to "tap" into our full potential.

Where does that leave God? If your full potential is already within you, then God becomes irrelevant. You don't need His transformative spirit. You don't need His guidance or forgiveness. You don't need Him.

It is true—you do have potential. You have amazing potential, b*ut it is not inherently within you.* It has been given to you and me by a loving Father, and we need Him to realize that full potential.

The path of *divine* intentionality is about letting go of trying to find happiness and self-fulfillment by ourselves. Instead, it's about seeking God's purpose for you, and then actively and *intentionally* pursuing that. It's about finding peace and happiness, not through the self, but through your relationship with God. He wants to be involved in your life. He wants to see you achieve your full potential. He wants you to *thrive*.

When you understand this, you will see a *bridge* to the other path that lies ahead. Beforehand, the new path may have seemed unreachable—too many changes, too much work, too much disruption to your life. The bridge makes that path accessible. It is your transitional period as you begin surrendering your will for God's.

It won't be easy. I can't tell you how long the bridge is. I *can* say that you will discover things about yourself that you don't like, because you will take things—things that kept you stuck for so long—with you (for a while anyway). You will still be in relationships that aren't always the healthiest, with people who might want to slow your progress or drag you back to their own familiar paths. You may even turn around and head back a ways or need to stop and remind yourself why you're on the bridge at all. It takes time to shed your old self and embrace the new path you've embarked on (Ephesians 4:22–24).

That's normal. All of us have great *intentions* when we first set out on our bridge toward that new path, but none of us live our intentions perfectly or continuously.

Part of the transitional period on the bridge is understanding your unique, God-given role as a woman, and the gifts and abilities you've been endowed with. It's also a time to reflect honestly about who will benefit, besides you, when you start to be more purposeful about life. What will change if you live with greater intention? How will it affect you and those around you and in what ways? Knowing your "why" is what will keep you moving down that bridge.

One thing I have learned through my own journey is that people can't always give me what I need, but God can. He is always there for me, always willing to listen to me. He loves me and cares about me deeply, as He does you. Be patient as you cross this bridge, because what's waiting for you on the other path is so much better.

Self-Worth That Lasts

One thing that's waiting for you is greater self-worth. If you were to look at yourself in the mirror and describe what you see, how would you do that? Do you *like* what you see? Do you feel *good* about what you see? Is that what determines your worth? It's pretty easy to see what's reflected back at you, but a mirror doesn't reflect what's *in* you, and what's in you is far more valuable than you may realize.

Self-worth and self-esteem are not the same. Self-esteem has to do with the way you perceive yourself. It often stems from external sources: your accomplishments, your children's accomplishments, how much money you have, how popular you are, how attractive you are, the way others treat you, etc. If you are honest with yourself about your strengths and weaknesses and don't rely too heavily on others' opinions, then it can be said that you have *healthy* self-esteem. Unhealthy self-esteem, however, can go one of two ways: having too high or too low of an opinion of yourself. The first can lead to narcissistic tendencies, the second to negative self-talk. Both give you a skewed perspective about where you fit in this world.

Self-worth is the knowledge that you are loveable and valuable, no matter how *capable* you are at something. Self-esteem fluctuates when it's standard of measurement is external, self-worth does not.

I'm a busy person. I like to be productive and I love using lists. I especially like crossing things off my list because it gives me a *temporary* sense of purpose and accomplishment. Unfortunately, it doesn't last. I set myself up for the never-ending cycle of having to *accomplish* just to feel good.

What I've learned is that real self-worth isn't accomplished by anything I do. Like most things, I've learned that the hard way. I've learned it by caring too much what others thought about me—caring more about people's opinions than God's.

If I could just be a better wife...

If I could just be a better therapist…
If I could just be a better friend…
If I could just be a better Christian…

I attached my worth to my productivity. Yet no matter how many women I helped, how many programs I created, or how many blogs I wrote, I still struggled to feel *worthwhile*.

It feels good to produce, of course. I enjoy the feeling of accomplishment when I finish a project or meet a goal. Those accomplishments, however, don't give me value in God's eyes. My worth actually comes from God—from His care and concern for me—and His purpose for me. I can't earn it. Therefore, my relationship with God is critical to my sense of worth. Without Him I'm stuck in that endless pursuit of things that bring only fleeting, momentary pleasure.

Changing paths moves me *away* from trying to do things on my own to feel accomplished or fulfilled. It moves me *toward* a greater dependency on God. Relying on Him instead of myself eliminates the discontent, stress, and frustration I feel day to day. It changes the way I feel when people don't live up to my expectations, or when I don't live up to God's expectations for me. Changing paths enables me to see my worth through God's eyes. It enables me to drown out all the noise from others and focus on Him. It brings me peace.

That's what's waiting for you if you switch paths.

Time to Choose

I'd like to say that choosing the intentional path was a quick and easy choice for me when things came to a head in 2013. It wasn't. It was a slow, arduous process that still isn't finished. It's been difficult—and painful—but worth it.

Are you ready to change your life? Are you ready to start living with full intention, as God has purposed for you? It's okay to be afraid. You don't have to wait for your fear to subside. You just have to have courage. That doesn't mean it will be easy, or obstacle-free. It will be hard. It will be challenging. It will be painful at times. Change anyway. It will be worth it!

WORKBOOK

Chapter One Questions

Question: How would you describe your *familiar* path? Be specific. What relationships are you in, and what choices are you (or others) making that are keeping you stuck?

_____
_____
_____
_____
_____
_____
_____
_____
_____
_____

Question: How would you change if you switched paths and took the one less traveled? How would your relationships change?

_____

_____

_____

_____

_____

_____

_____

_____

_____

Question: What's keeping you from crossing the bridge to the path less traveled? For example, fear of the unknown, finances, apathy, etc.?

_____

_____

_____

_____

_____

_____

Question: Have you ever felt close to God? Describe that time.

_____
_____
_____
_____
_____
_____
_____
_____
_____
_____

Question: What does God think about you? (Check out https://www.openbible.info/topics/self_worth for scriptures that address this.)

_____
_____
_____
_____
_____
_____

Action: Plan to spend time each day with God. Some people call this a "quiet time" or "devotion." A Bible and a journal or prayer notebook are helpful tools to establish a regular time with God.

Chapter One Notes

CHAPTER TWO

The Intentional Way

You have two choices. You can either live intentionally or you can live unintentionally.

Just ask Kara. Her life has been a revolving door of men that made her feel good for a season, then damaged her in countless ways. Her relationships with her grown children are a mess. None of them want anything to do with her. She's promised them the world, over and over, and failed to deliver repeatedly. She blames her childhood—and her ex-husbands. Her excessive drinking habit she learned from her dad, her chronic smoking from her mom. Her temper is genetic. Her obesity comes from her years of being victimized by sexual predators. Her inability to hold down the various jobs she's had is the result of others who just don't *understand*.

Kara is the quintessential example of a woman who is *not* living with intention. She says she wants to, but she has no idea what that even means.

Divinely intentional living *is*:

- Knowing *why* you exist. What plans and intentions does God have for you? How is that connected with what you do on a day-to-day basis?

- Having a *detailed vision* of what your life needs to look like *and* what it will look like beyond this lifetime.
- Living according to a set of beliefs and values that support your vision.
- Setting proactive goals based on those beliefs and values.
- Making daily choices that turn into habits, which, in turn, support your goals.
- Making each moment move you in a purposeful direction. That means, making time for self-reflection. Yet many people seem to have a hard time being alone with their thoughts. We often fill up our downtime with work or entertainment instead.
- Taking responsibility for every choice you make and owning the consequences that ensue.

Divinely intentional living is *not*:

- A rigid, inflexible plan for life. Life's going to throw you curve balls and you need to be able to handle them when they come your way—without getting hit in the face.
- Living on autopilot.
- Blaming others for missed opportunities or unhappy circumstances.
- Taking care of others to the exclusion of self.

- Living without a blueprint for life.

The first choice—to live with intention—is the best. It's not the easiest though. Living with intention is *hard*. The path less traveled still has obstacles to overcome. You will face resistance when you make changes—from yourself as well as from others. This new path is also unfamiliar, which makes it scary. You don't know what's coming, which is an uncomfortable, even terrifying, feeling. You will also make mistakes as you venture down this new path—mistakes that may lead to new hurts and disappointments.

What's different about this new path then?

You!

You may not be like Kara. You might feel fulfilled in some ways. You may not have suffered abuse or have chronic bad habits that drag you down. There's another way, however, that *unintentionality* can creep in.

Do you ever feel like your day consists of waking up, running around all day long, only to fall into bed exhausted at the end of it? Do you wonder what you've actually accomplished? I know I do. Sometimes I feel like one of those hamsters, spinning around and around in its wheel, but never actually going anywhere. I don't like that feeling. I'm moving constantly, juggling all kinds of roles and responsibilities, but for what? Where does it all lead? Did I even choose to go there?

Too many women are just going through the motions. They're busy, but not purposeful. And that's not okay. It's certainly not what God intended. Being too busy to be intentional doesn't lead to an abundant life. It leads to stress and overwhelm.

There's a huge difference between just getting by and living with divine intention. We're driven to produce, to be productive. But the faster we go and the harder we push, the more stressed out we become. There's very little peace of mind these days, very little joy or contentment with life. We pursue feelings of pleasure and gratification, which we label happiness. But at the same time, anxiety and depression appear to be on the rise.

When you decide to live with intention, your mindset changes. You learn to identify unhealthy habits, distorted thinking, negative coping behaviors. You learn tools that will change your perceptions and reactions to situations. You stop making excuses for setbacks. You stop blaming circumstances. You know where you want to go, and you take responsibility for how you do that (and how long it takes you).

Your behaviors change too. You become mindful about what you're doing and why. You convert "busyness" into purposefulness. Your dreams become your intentions, which in turn become your goals.

Intentional living from a divine perspective is what brings peace of mind—true peace, not just the absence of conflict.

The Unintentional Way

Failure to live intentionally can cause problems in every aspect of our life.

Take Denise for example. When she first came to see me, she was frazzled and overwhelmed. She struggled with anxiety, self-doubt, and insecurity about her capabilities, her weight, even her desirability. On top of all that, Denise had a hard time saying "no" to people. She was stretched thin with too many responsibilities and not enough time. She had responsibilities at home, at work, and at church, as well as various volunteer projects she'd taken on.

Yet she found it hard to delegate things. She was always tired, and lately she'd been noticing that she was "losing it" with her kids—yelling at them more for things that were really inconsequential.

Her children and her job took up a large part of her day. She and her husband hardly talked about anything except the kids, bills, and day-to-day routine topics. She was also feeling resentful toward her husband because she felt he didn't help her enough around the house. But she didn't know how to talk to him without getting angry, even though she realized it was impacting their relationship. She knew he was feeling neglected, but what could she do? She was too tired for conversation most of the time. She couldn't even remember the last time they'd had sex.

Denise is not alone. Many studies show that women can begin to neglect their marriages over time as the demands of child-rearing take over.[1] They're exhausted. They worry excessively about everything and fail to handle their thoughts or emotions well, repeating the same behaviors but hoping for different outcomes. How does Denise change this?

How do *you*?

Get Your Priorities Right

Life is about relationships. They are essential to our well-being because they keep us connected, give us support, and help us maintain balance and a healthy perspective on things.

They keep us motivated to stay on the right path.

Not all relationships are equal, however.

Denise wanted to live with greater intention (it was why she'd come to see me in the first place). But she didn't know how, and she certainly didn't know why. She thought she did, though. She thought it was because she wanted to be happier. She wanted better communication with her husband. She wanted to stop yelling at her kids. She wanted to feel better about herself. What she came to realize was that her biggest reasons for living with intention had to do with two relationships she'd been ignoring up to that point—her relationship with God and with herself.

The same is true for you and me.

The first step towards the intentional living path is to prioritize your relationships.

The most important relationship you have is with God, because only He can secure your ultimate future, the one beyond this lifetime. Investing in your relationship with God lays the foundation for building a meaningful life *and* helps prepare you for what's beyond.

Pursuits that aren't God-centered are ultimately empty. They may bring fleeting moments of pleasure that resemble happiness, but you can't sustain them. Without Him you're just spinning your wheels.

Denise came to see that even though she talked about God needing to be first in her life, in reality she struggled to find the time to pray and study His Word. She *wanted* to, but she had a lot of excuses. She was too tired, there were too many demands on her time, she didn't know what to say to God, and she was afraid He was too disappointed in her to listen anyway.

She kept up appearances. She went to church. She served. She sang in the choir. She tried to teach her children about God. Yet all the while she struggled to see her value from God's perspective because she wasn't getting to know Him intimately. She wasn't building a personal relationship with Him, so she didn't really *know* Him. She didn't know that she could trust Him, lean on Him, and turn to Him with all her struggles. She didn't realize that He *wanted* her to do that. Instead, she was trying to handle everything herself.

The second most important relationship you have is with yourself. It's not because you come first. It's because there are people in your life who love you and need you to be healthy, in every possible way.

That means you need to take care of yourself.

Denise struggled with self-care, because it felt selfish. She believed that if she took time for herself then she would have to sacrifice someone else's needs. She came to see, over time, that she'd been waiting for her family to respect her, to see her needs and go out of their way to meet them. They weren't, and it wasn't their job to do that. It was hers.

Her inability to see the value she has in God's eyes kept her from placing value on her own personal well-being. She gave and gave to others and wondered why she was feeling resentful.

Denise had to see that self-care is *essential* to divinely intentional living. If the God of the entire universe (and beyond) wants to have a relationship with her, then *she must be precious to Him*. She must be worth taking care of.

Once Denise prioritized her relationships, her attitude shifted, and her marriage improved as a result. Putting God first changed her perspective in a healthy way. Though prayer and Bible study didn't "fix" her problems, they helped her to see that God does care about her and knows her struggles. Over time she began looking for opportunities to change things about herself: the way she responded to people, the way she viewed situations, and the way she managed herself and her emotions. With each adjustment she made in her thinking and her actions, she began to see positive outcomes.

Determine Your "Why"

The second step towards the intentional living path is to determine what your motivations are.

You're tired of walking aimlessly down that familiar path and you know you need to make some changes. You want something better, and you've made a decision to put God first and take better care of yourself. That's great, but why? That may seem like a silly question, but it's probably the most important.

Let me put it this way. Let's say you want to lose ten pounds so you can fit into *that* dress. You know, the one you wore for a special occasion a while ago that's hiding at the back of your closet? There's no way you're getting it on right now, but if you could just fit into it, you could feel happy about yourself again. You would feel confident about your body, which would carry over to every other aspect of your life.

You make a plan. You go on a diet. You begin working out, and the weight starts to come off. You feel so proud of yourself. People are noticing and complimenting you. You look into the mirror every day and see a slimmer version of yourself emerging, and you determine that this time the weight will *stay* off. Eventually you get into that dress again.

Then the months go by. Maybe a year or two has passed, and now you've gained all that weight back plus five, or ten, pounds.

What happened? How could you forget the way it felt to accomplish your goal, to make the changes you committed to with such determination?

The problem goes back to my original question. *Why* did you want to lose the weight to begin with? Your short-term goal to fit into your dress was a powerful motivator, but it wasn't enough to sustain the changes you made. Once you accomplished your goal your motivation to continue diminished. Not at first, but slowly. The diet you were on became a little too hard to maintain. Exceptions, little by little, became incorporated back into your eating habits. The extreme exercise regime became harder to sustain and over time you found reasons to not work out as much. Until, finally, you were hardly exercising at all.

Your good intentions of maintaining your weight loss faded away.

Motivation is an interesting thing. It's the reason *why* we do things, and why we *keep* doing them. I've learned, personally and professionally, that we rarely stay motivated to continue behaviors for a goal with a deadline that's come and gone, *if that was our only motivator*. In order to stay motivated once the original goal has been met, we must set a new one—a new, equally motivating reason for sustaining our new habits.

Choosing a new path is no different. If your short-term motivation, for example, is to improve a relationship, change jobs, or stop engaging in addictive behaviors, then what happens when you've done that? What keeps you moving down the better path?

That's why it's so important to know *why* you want to live with intention, and why God wants you to.

Remember, it's not all about you. Who, besides you, will benefit and in what ways?

At the same time, being intentional means you know where you're going and why you want to go there. While you will accomplish goals along the way, *you aren't done living intentionally until you're done living*—your motivation needs to carry you all the way.

Become Intentional with Your Time

The third step in choosing the intentional living path is to make time.

When we were young girls, it seemed we had all the time in the world. We know differently now. We know that time won't be around forever. That means every moment counts!

Look around. You have the same amount of time as

everyone else, which means you have equal opportunity to use it wisely. Do you? Do you use time to move you in the direction you want to go, or does time get wasted?

No woman I know manages herself perfectly. I certainly don't. But every intentional woman I know realizes that managing time is actually about managing yourself. That means, knowing when you are at your optimal best in the day and when you are not. It means using tools to help you become and stay organized. It means being balanced in how you distribute your time to the people in your life.

Life is filled with distractions that will steer you away from your new path. Zig Ziglar, businessman, author and motivational speaker, once said "Lack of direction, not lack of time, is the problem. We all have twenty-four hour days." What distracts you? Take inventory for a few days of all the ways you were distracted from your intentions. Were they worth it? What price did you (and others) pay as a result?

Saying "I don't have time" is an excuse for the lazy—for the ones who don't want to do the hard work that intentional living requires. Yes, as I've said already, intentional living is hard. It's also incredibly rewarding.

Live with Passion

To walk the intentional path, you must prioritize your relationships. You must know *why* you want to be on that path to start with. And you must use time with purpose.

There's one more step to finding and walking that beautiful, divinely intentional path—*passion!*

If you've lost your zeal for life, I get it. Things get you down. You get weary of the mundane, overwhelmed by responsibilities, disappointed and discouraged by people and situations.

To live intentionally you must *love to live!* You must

embrace everything that comes your way, even the hard things. That means finding:

- Joy in the midst of chaos
- Peace in the midst of turmoil
- Contentment in the face of uncertainty

Know the difference between fleeting moments of happiness versus the sheer exhilaration that comes from throwing everything you have into living with intention!

Those who have a real zest for life aren't those who haven't suffered or struggled less. They are those who have learned to effectively *incorporate* those struggles and sufferings into a full life.

Be the Best Version of Yourself

One last thing.

When a woman is living intentionally, she is her best self. She lives in the moment, but with an eye to the future. She is aware of how her choices impact others. She knows there are things she can't control, but she can choose how to think and feel about them. She can choose how to respond to them. Though she feels fear at times, she doesn't allow herself to react out of fear or to be bound by it. She doesn't justify her mistakes. She acknowledges them and then tries to do better.

When a woman is living intentionally, she is thinking about what she wants her life to look like, about what

God wants it to look like, and then moves herself in that direction.

WORKBOOK

Chapter Two Questions

Question: Looking over the lists of what intentional living is and what it is not, in what ways are you living intentionally? In what ways are you missing out on an intentional life? Are you living life with passion, or just going through the motions?

_____

_____

_____

_____

_____

_____

_____

_____

_____

_____

Question: How are you currently prioritizing your relationships? How are you spending your time to reflect those priorities?

_____
_____
_____
_____
_____
_____
_____
_____
_____
_____

Question: Who will benefit from you living with greater intention?

_____
_____
_____
_____
_____
_____

Question: How are you currently prioritizing your relationships? How are you spending your time to reflect those priorities?

_____

_____

_____

_____

_____

_____

_____

_____

_____

_____

Action: Jot down words or phrases that come to mind when you think about the life God wants for you, and that you want to create for yourself. You will use these in the following chapters.

_____

_____

_____

_____

_____

Chapter Two Notes

CHAPTER THREE

Intentionality and Intimacy

Relationships are tough. It's easy to come away from them with mixed messages about yourself—some positive, some negative. All of them are integral to how intentional your life will be.

There's an innate truth about relationships: the more time and effort you put into them, the greater the intimacy. The path of intentionality requires intimacy. So if you want to change your life, you have to change your relationships.

I'm not talking about your marriage, though that may need changing too. I'm not talking about having a better relationship with your children, your parents, your siblings, or your friends.

I'm talking about getting to know God—really know Him—and getting to know yourself. It's impossible to be divinely intentional about life without both, and there's no shortcut to intimacy. You have to put in the time and effort to develop an intimate bond.

That can be challenging, however.

The Making of a Woman

I grew up in British Columbia, the oldest of three girls. My parents were both teachers, and though we lived in a city, virtually every school break was spent outdoors, camping, hunting, and fishing. From an early age, wilderness skills were part of our education. I knew how to handle guns long before I could successfully navigate a curling iron, and my expertise with a canoe far surpassed my social skills with peers.

Part of that was because I was a quiet child. My quiet nature was reinforced considerably through my elementary school years, which were difficult. I started school at age five, but because of the way my birthday fell my parents decided to put me straight into first grade instead of kindergarten. That may not seem like a big deal, but it really had a huge impact. First of all, all the other children were older. They'd already experienced a year of school, whereas I knew nothing about what to expect. I didn't know any of my peers, and to make matters more difficult, I was a late transfer since we'd moved one month after school started.

I'll never forget one incident early on that shaped my thinking in a big way. Mrs. McClellan, my first-grade teacher, got angry at one of my classmates in front of all of us, because he had forgotten to bring a snack for recess—the details are a little fuzzy, of course. I'm not sure how she found out, or even why she made such a fuss about it, but it made him cry. I was terrified of also getting in trouble because I didn't have a snack either, so I ate my tomato sandwich which left me without a lunch. Then I walked home at lunch time, only to get in trouble with my mother.

That taught me at the tender age of five that complying was important. I didn't like getting in trouble. It also taught me that it was better to not call attention to myself.

The next year when we moved again and I started Grade Two at a new school, those lessons were firmly fixed in my brain. As happens to so many children, it was reinforced by school bullies—and teachers who did nothing. The first day of school every fall was especially difficult because I never knew what class I would be in for the year until I showed up that first morning.

A list would be posted on the front doors for all grades: your assignment of teacher, room, and classmates. I always felt dread that first day, not knowing who would be in my class. Seats weren't assigned, so I would select one on the farthest aisle closest to a wall, where I could be relatively invisible.

Yet kids still found me in the hallways, bathrooms, playgrounds. They called me names, occasionally pushed me, and made fun of my clothes. They certainly didn't want to hang out with me. I was rarely invited over to other kids' homes. I dreaded times when the P.E. teacher would appoint captains and they would pick their teams, because I was invariably the last standing.

I learned to hide—not literally but within the pages of books, which I much preferred to conversation. I didn't make friends easily and was possessive of the one or two I had. Books though, they were my friend. They allowed me to escape to another, safer world; a world that didn't require me to interact.

Yet other things were shaping me too, positive things.

Fathers and Daughters

Little girls need their father, so do big girls. Not all fathers are equal though. As dads go, mine was a very good one.

From a very young age, I was learning survival skills that most children my age weren't. I learned how to start fires without matches, navigate class IV rapids in the stern of a canoe, use a compass, read a topographical map, skin an animal, and build a snow cave to survive a winter's night in if I had to.

Dad taught me those things. He taught me to face challenges by putting me in situations that weren't always easy or comfortable. Pulling a boat through tall, swampy weeds is not pleasant. Nor is sleeping on unlevel ground with rocks underneath you or being swept broadside down a fast-moving river and almost capsizing. I can't begin to tell you how many times I had to face up to my fear of heights as I traversed over steep, narrow mountain passes while backpacking, or rode shotgun in the jeep on uneven switchbacks with steep drop-offs. Sometimes I was so scared that I'd just get out of the vehicle and walk.

My sisters and I weren't allowed to be squeamish. The fact that we weren't boys was never an excuse. Gutting a fish without worrying about my fingernails became a source of pride. I pitied girls who cared only about dresses and hairstyles and makeup. Learning to do things that Dad liked was far more important at the time.

It wasn't always easy though. Dad was tough; he certainly wasn't interested in raising wimps. He wanted strong, confident, capable girls—girls who could take care of themselves if need be. He was constantly giving us opportunities to grow and learn.

He founded the Outdoors Club and the Ski Club at the junior high school he taught at, so that when my sisters and I were old enough, we could participate. I learned how to ski because of that. For two years, every Thursday night after school club members would be bused to Grouse Mountain where we'd take night ski lessons.

He initiated the Duke of Edinburgh[2] program in our youth group at church, and then required me and my sisters to be among the first to achieve the various levels. That meant planning our own wilderness expeditions, without adult supervision, among many other requirements.

He coached me in track, which I excelled at. As I got better, he would push me to improve. He'd make me train twice a day: early morning and as soon as I got home from school. He'd have me train at the same time as the Kajaks, a high-performance track and field team in Richmond, BC. Their workouts were so difficult that I couldn't keep up. I would often feel nauseous afterwards, but just trying pushed me to a higher level of ability.

Because of Dad, I learned mental toughness and fortitude. I learned perseverance. I learned to set goals, plan ahead, and to look beyond immediate boundaries—to never let them overcome me. Anytime I faced something tough I would remind myself of who I was. I was strong. I was capable. I was determined. Dad didn't pump us up with false flattery or set us up with unrealistic expectations of life. Instead he used his love of the outdoors to teach us what life is like and who God is.

He wasn't perfect though. My dad wasn't much of a talker when I was child. We could travel for hours in the same vehicle without any conversation. Perhaps that's because he'd had his own difficult childhood, which I didn't find out about until many years later. Perhaps it's just that he's a quiet man.

Sometimes Dad's love felt conditional. If I did the things he wanted, in the way he wanted, then he was pleased with me. If I trained hard and ran well, if I learned skills that he valued, if I was respectful and obedient—then I could bask in the warmth of his approval.

Sometimes, though, he could be overly critical and short-tempered. I feared his anger, even though I was learning to be independent. I craved words of encouragement, especially from Dad. Yet he was often terse about what he wanted and why.

It was a strange dichotomy. On the one hand, I was learning to stand on my own two feet. On the other, I was struggling socially to fit in with my peers. I cared about what people thought, about pleasing them.

Adults seemed to love me because I was polite, respectful, and rule-abiding. While other kids were rebelling, I was complying. I wanted a voice, but I wasn't strong enough to risk displeasing anyone.

Even though I was gaining skills and characteristics that would serve me well in years to come, I didn't have the self-confidence to see it at the time. My ability to express myself, to relate to others, was lacking. The message I was taking away from childhood wasn't that I was competent, but that I didn't fit in. I was different.

Few wanted to be my friend because I wasn't interested in doing things that might get me in trouble. Nor was I allowed to. Mom and Dad were strict, for which I am deeply grateful, because they protected me from my own potential foolishness. That strictness, however, also set me apart from my peers.

A Different Father

Everything matters. Everything has meaning. The things that happened to you when you were still a young girl stay with you. They make an indelible mark on your soul.

Not all girls are lucky to have a father like I have. Some grow up with dads who didn't teach them anything. Some grow up with no dad at all. When a girl is repeatedly told that she is ugly by her peers, she grows up believing it. When she is told that she is stupid, she stops trying to excel. When no one invites her over, or she is chosen last, she begins to question her worth. When no one chooses her at all, she pulls inside herself.

Then that girl becomes a woman. She tells herself those things aren't true and to a certain extent she may believe that. Life experiences help her gain some self-assurance.

Other experiences trigger that inner voice that's still nagging at her, reminding her of her inadequacies. Those voices shape her decisions. They also shape her understanding of another father-daughter relationship. They certainly shaped mine.

I've worked with countless women who struggle with insecurities. They may believe in God, yet they don't feel close to Him. They undoubtedly don't feel valuable. Nor do they see Him as a loving Father.

That says a lot about the inadequacies of our imperfect, physical fathers. How can you see God as tender, compassionate, and loving if your own father wasn't even present, or if he was around, he was distant, critical, harsh, or just ineffectual?

Dads matter and having a lousy dad or no dad at all shapes a woman in a myriad of ways. It also affects her ability to see God as He is.

Your Heavenly Father wants to know you, and for you to know Him, because He has a tremendous purpose and plan for you. He's the perfect Father, in every way, and He loves you more than you can possibly know. He wants a close relationship with you, but for that to happen, you have to want it. You have to believe you can have it. You have to invest in it.

If you weren't close to your physical father, that may be difficult. It may be hard to see God for the loving, nurturing Father that He is because you may be superimposing qualities of your physical father onto Him. If everything you think you know about fathers was shaped by the one who raised you (or didn't), then it's going to be tough to get past that.

How can you see God as your best friend—the one you go to with your most difficult problems—if your physical father caused more problems than he solved? How can you trust that God will always listen when your dad ignored you? How can you see God as one who will comfort you and then gently guide you to see what you need to see, so that you can grow to be more intentional?

I never doubted my father's love for me, ever. He told me often, and he showed me in a myriad of ways. I struggled to *communicate* with God, however, because I couldn't communicate with Dad. I saw God as only being able to love me if I did everything *right*. If I screwed up, made bad choices, then God must be deeply disappointed with me. He certainly wouldn't want a relationship with someone as flawed as me.

I tried to pray and read my Bible because it was the right thing to do. It's how I'd been taught, but I wasn't *used* to talking and I didn't know how to open up. I didn't see the value in it, and I didn't think He'd want to listen.

It was many years before I came to desire a relationship with Him or know how to build one. I needed to understand that He's always been there, waiting for me to realize it, waiting for me to just start talking. I didn't mind listening to Him (reading the Bible) but I wasn't holding up my end of the relationship at all.

That relationship didn't happen quickly; it was a process, and it's not over. Some days I am a better daughter than others.

The divinely intentional path starts with you seeking a loving father-daughter relationship with God. You need Him if you're going to be intentional about life, if you're going to stay on the right path.

How do you need Him?

- You need to know how much you matter to Him.

- You need to know that He has a *plan* for you.

- You need His love, mercy, compassion, peace of mind, forgiveness.

- You need His protection from dangerous situations.
- You need His healing, for physical and emotional aches.
- You need to know that no matter how short you fall from perfection, He will always love you.

There is nothing you can do that will ever make God stop loving you. That doesn't mean He's always proud of your choices, or that there won't be consequences attached to them. It means, however, that no matter what you've done—what you will do—God's love is unswerving. He'll always be waiting for you with open arms (Romans 8:38–39).

These days it's God's love for me that pushes and pulls me through the ups and downs of life; it inspires me to keep going when I want to give up. It tells me that life is worth investing in; that *I am* worth investing in. Do you believe that God loves *you* that much?

A Relationship Worth Investing In

Part of choosing to live with greater intention from a divine perspective means coming to know yourself intimately. It means asking God to help you see yourself as He sees you. He knows you aren't perfect, but He still wants you to strive for perfection (Matthew 5:48). Yet He wants you to have a realistic self-view, not a distorted perspective about your own greatness, nor your own unworthiness. Both are counterproductive.

As with so many women, my path of self-discovery has occurred in short spurts throughout my life. Graduate school was undoubtedly the first place I was really forced to take a good look at myself. That was because I lived alone, and I was deeply lonely.

I had just finished college in East Texas, where I attended a private Christian university. My degree was in Theology, with an emphasis in Psychology. Rather than returning to Canada, I chose to continue my education in Texas.

I knew I wanted to be a counselor, though I discovered this circuitously. My original intent had been to follow in the path of both my parents, as a teacher. Then, briefly, I thought I wanted to be in Public Relations. It wasn't until I read a book on Art Therapy the summer after my junior year, that I knew I'd found my career path.

Graduate school was challenging—not academically, but in personal ways. I'd moved out of a dorm where I was surrounded by friends and social opportunities, and into a small house of my own in a different town. I didn't have a television or personal computer. Cell phones didn't exist. I was by myself.

Classes were fascinating, however. I was the youngest in the program at 22. Many of my classmates were married (or divorced) and already working in related fields. Even though I made new friends, most had families to go home to at the end of the day.

I excelled academically and when it came time to do my internship I was selected—with a small handful of my peers—for a coveted position at the community mental health center. It was also the first time I saw my own counselor. Even though it wasn't a requirement of the program, we were encouraged to experience therapy as clients. It turned out to be one of the best things I have ever done. It put me on a path of self-awareness and self-improvement that has become a lifelong quest. That was only the beginning of my journey.

When we come to understand just how much God

loves us, it changes our relationship with ourselves. At least, it ought to. Everything that you are, everything that you are capable of, everything *good* about you, comes from God.

God tells you to love others *as you love yourself* (Mark 12:30–31). But what if you struggle with deep-seated insecurities, even self-loathing? How can you love others, or love life, if you hate who you are? Wrong choices—and the byproduct of them—are a part of the human existence. We all have scars. That's what sin does. It leaves big, gaping wounds in us that don't always heal properly. Hate sin, certainly—and the hurt that wrong choices have caused you and others. Don't, however, hate yourself. God created you and He loves His creation (Genesis 1:31).

When I began working with the university counselor, I was asked some tough questions:

What do you value about yourself?

What do you not value about yourself?

Those were hard for me to answer. I'd never reflected on those things before. Now, suddenly, I was being asked to do so. I found it easy to say what I didn't like but I hadn't been raised to focus on my strengths. Doing so might lead to pride and vanity, or so I'd been taught. Instead, my focus had always been on how I *didn't measure up*.

Discouragement and feeling like a failure are two sure ways to pull you back to your familiar path in a hurry. Self-entitlement and self-gratification don't do us any favors either. Some women grow up in environments where they are spoiled and pampered. Others face untold hardships. Both lead to distorted thinking.

True intimacy with yourself requires honesty, which

takes time. It takes getting quiet and reflecting on the choices you've made and where those choices have brought you. Before you can determine where you need to go, you must know where you are now and how you got here.

For me that meant a lot of journaling. I began writing everything down: my thoughts, feelings, hopes, and dreams. I used the time alone to begin getting to know myself.

It was hard and painful. But in looking at myself honestly, dispassionately—accepting the good and acknowledging the imperfect—a plan began to form. I could identify areas of my life that I wanted to change or improve. I could begin investing in myself.

Do you believe you're worth investing in?

You are special. You are worthwhile. It may not feel that way at times. You may not have been treated that way by your earthly parents or others, but it's true nonetheless.

God has invested in you, so you need to as well. Self-investment is essential to an intentional life *and* is beneficial to your loved ones. When you place value on yourself, they will too. That means putting your time, energy, passion, and sometimes your money where your *intentions* are.

You can't invest in yourself if you *don't know who you are*. You can't ask others to invest in you if you're not willing to invest in yourself.

Busy Isn't Always Better

One indication that you're on the wrong path is when your relationships with others are not intentionally moving you toward God's purpose and plan for you. If you are in unhealthy, unbalanced, even abusive relationships, then it's going to be difficult—perhaps even impossible—to live with divine intention. Those relationships will have a toxic impact on your thinking which will, in turn, affect every choice you make.

That doesn't mean you have to leave the relationship. It does mean, however, that you must recognize your part in how and why there are problems, and then work to change that. It may also mean that you need to ask for change in the other person.

Anytime you ask others to care for you, care about what you think feel and do, you are asking them to invest—to care about you, make time for you, respect and appreciate what you have to offer. They ask the same of you. Relationships which have that kind of give-and-take are much healthier and stronger. There is a balance, a mutual reliance on each other. That means you have to be confident about the relationship without losing your identity. You love being with that person, but you're able to function without them.

Another challenge to having intentional relationships is that we're just so busy. We rush here and there, pursuing our passions, hopes, dreams and goals. We try to get ahead, accomplish, and improve our circumstances yet move further away from what really brings us life satisfaction—our connections with people.

The world can be a lonely place. Even in a crowded room it's easy to feel alone, like no one notices you, no one cares. If that's true for you, ask yourself some important questions as you think about how intentional you are about the relationships you have.

- What am I pursuing that I value more than my relationships?
- Which is more important? To pursue my own passions or to pursue greater intimacy with others?

- Do my loved ones feel loved by me or used?
- What would change if I made my relationships the center of my life, instead of something I squeezed into the crevices of my life?

It's impossible to give everyone the same amount of time, or the same quality of time. You have to prioritize because *not all relationships are equal*. That means that the people who mean the most to you need to know *the most* that they matter.

If you want to live with divine intention, you must have intimate connections with people. But it's up to *you* to make that happen—first God, then you, then others.

WORKBOOK

Chapter Three Questions

Question: What kind of relationship did/do you have with your physical father? How has that impacted your relationship with God?

_____
_____
_____
_____
_____
_____
_____
_____
_____
_____
_____
_____

Question: What do you value about yourself? What do you not value?

_____
_____
_____
_____
_____
_____
_____
_____
_____
_____

Question: Do you have intimacy with God? What would your life look like if you did? What do you believe God's purpose is for you?

_____
_____
_____
_____
_____
_____

Question: Do your other relationships reflect the kind of intimacy you want? If not, why not?

Action: What intentions will you make this next week, to build greater intimacy with God and others?

Chapter Three Notes

CHAPTER FOUR

What's the Point?

What gets you up every morning? Besides the obvious, of course (no, not coffee—okay, maybe coffee). Whether you work outside of the home or not, there's so much to do. In addition to your other responsibilities, maybe there are children to get fed, dressed, and off to school; a house to clean at some point; laundry to be cleaned and put away; groceries to be bought; meals to be cooked.

It can be exhausting to think about anything beyond the day-to-day, so sometimes we don't. The alarm goes off, our feet hit the ground, and we're moving—all day long. But has anything we've done that day moved us toward our life's purpose? Do you even know what that is? Where do you go to find out?

Your purpose is what gives you a direction to move in—where you want to go, who you want to be—who you *need* to be. It helps you sort through the *busyness* of life so that you can make the most of it. It ensures that your daily decisions are intentionally moving you in a purposeful direction. God has a definite purpose for you. How do you figure out what that purpose is and if you're truly living it? To understand your God-given purpose, you must first understand that His purpose is *greater* than any of the roles you fill right now.

What Defines You?

Most women imagine what their future life will be like when they're young. They dream of getting married, having a family, of making a difference in the world. So, what does it mean when one or more of those opportunities doesn't present itself?

I thought my purpose was to get married and have children. In fact, I had it all figured out. I was going to have four children, be a stay-at-home mom who worked part-time and homeschooled—but that didn't happen.

Though many years have passed, I can still recall the events that led up to both of my miscarriages. I was 31 when I became pregnant the first time. We'd waited for four years before trying, and then—as it happens—it took me a year to get pregnant. I was only a month along, and I had been dealing with sharp pains all week. My husband and I were traveling home from a friend's house where we had spent the weekend. About halfway home, I knew something was very wrong, so we drove straight to the nearest hospital. A sonogram revealed that the pregnancy was ectopic; the embryo had attached to my fallopian tube instead of my uterus. I was prepped for immediate surgery.

It was an overwhelming time. Everything was happening at once, with no time to really comprehend it. It wasn't until days afterward that the reality of losing the pregnancy fully hit. Yet I hadn't given up on the idea that I would be a mother. My idea of who I was meant to be as a woman—who I wanted to be—was completely wrapped up in having children.

It took two years for me to get pregnant again. This time we made it to the 11th week before I miscarried. I had already had a sonogram to make sure everything was okay, but I began to worry anyway. My morning sickness had abruptly stopped a few days earlier and I remember confiding in a friend at work that I was afraid this might mean something was wrong. She assured me that things were probably fine. They weren't.

That pregnancy was many years ago; it was to be our last.

I never expected to be one of those women who would never have children. There was never a point where I just said, "I'm not going to be a mom. Oh well." We never stopped trying and I never stopped thinking about it. We even attempted to adopt a child. We paid money to an agency, spent hours putting together a birth profile, and met with a social worker to do a home study. Then we waited. And waited. And waited. We were never selected.

Gradually, over time, I came to the realization that my life was taking a very different path than I'd ever expected.

I struggled with some fundamental questions:

Wasn't it my purpose in life to be a mother?

Have I failed to fulfill my purpose?

What now?

Sometimes we do that. We confuse our roles with God's purpose for us. When a certain role that we've longed for doesn't come about, we can question whether our purpose in life has passed us by.

Do you believe you're failing to fulfill *your* purpose because of some unfulfilled role? Are you letting your roles *define* who you are? People who don't know you well can still describe you pretty accurately—the things that describe you are things that others can see with their eyes. They can also get a sense of who you are by knowing the functional roles you have as a woman, a wife, a mom, an employee.

People may also make judgments about you based on their own value system. Some will say you should look a certain way. Others will say that certain roles are more important or valuable than others. Are all wives the same? Mothers? Daughters? Employees? Friends? Your roles don't define you—it's how you *conduct* yourself in those roles that defines you.

What defines you ought to be internal—your character, the choices you make, and the values you live by. You are defined by what you believe and value about human life, and by *God's* intent for you now and later. Your roles are constantly shifting and changing as time goes by. So does your function, your *job description,* within each of those roles. If you let yourself be defined by your roles, and then some roles end or change, you will be disappointed. When you let others tell you what to value or not, then they get to *define* you instead of doing it for yourself.

Finding Fulfillment

Katrina is a friend of mine who has wrestled with this—deciding what defines her—for many years. She'd always been very goal oriented. As a young woman, with her whole life ahead of her, she had a very specific plan written out for her future. She even wrote it out in a memory book for high school seniors. "At 17 you think everything's going to go the way you want it. The way you plan it," she shared with me. She thought that if she wrote out, in detail, every step of the life she wanted, then it would happen that way. Part of her plan was to be a wife and mother by the age of 35. But 35 came and went. She was still single.

"I struggled for a long time," she told me. "I felt like I was a failure. I wasn't accomplishing anything. I wasn't following the plan. And it's almost like society expects that of you too. So it heightens your disappointment in yourself, your sense of failure. The longer I went unmarried, the more people would notice and comment, which only made it worse."

When she heard, "Katrina I just don't understand why God hasn't made you a mother yet and blessed you with children," it reinforced that she must be doing something wrong.

When people said, "I'm praying for you to find a husband," she knew they meant well. But it implied that there was something missing or wrong with her life.

"Those comments only validated all the negative self-talk I already had in my head. I didn't know where I fit in the world if I wasn't where I thought I was going to be, or where I should be. And I really struggled with God. I didn't understand why He wasn't blessing me in the ways I expected. I felt like I was doing all the right things but still not being blessed."

Katrina finally came to a turning point. "I realized that the plan I had written for myself wasn't necessarily God's. That just because I wasn't married with children didn't mean I didn't have purpose. That was a lie I'd been telling myself. I've done so much, accomplished so much."

Katrina couldn't see those things because she was confusing the roles in life she'd hoped to have with God's purpose for her. Once Katrina saw that her life still had meaning, she was able to start turning her thinking around. She came to see that she had to make daily decisions that reflected that purpose.

"I'm trying to intentionally speak the truth to myself that I have a great life, a great purpose. And that I am able to do so much more by focusing on what God has in store for me than focusing on what I don't have. He *has* blessed me, in His way, according to His plan."

Katrina's roles are different than she thought they would be, but she's come to realize that through it all, her purpose *never* changed.

Knowing Your Purpose

So now we come to the million-dollar question: What *is* your God-given purpose?

Millions of people struggle with the question, "Why am I here? What does it all mean?" Even people who profess Christianity don't all agree. A woman's purpose is the same as a man's in terms of being a Christian—that is, your purpose is gender-neutral. It is *your reason for being born*, and it can only be found through God's Word. The Bible doesn't reveal all the answers about what our existence will be like beyond this life, but it does give some interesting glimpses into an incredible future.

What does the Bible say?

- We are told to seek first God's Kingdom and His righteousness (Matthew 6:33).
- To grow in the grace and knowledge of Jesus Christ (II Peter 3:18).
- We know that those who have God's Spirit produce fruit (Galatians 5:22–23).

Using those basic concepts, we can begin to understand our primary purpose as Christian women by discovering the following:

- What is God's Kingdom, and what role might I play in that?
- How might my current functions and my God-given talents and abilities be preparing me for that future role?

- What does His righteousness look like, and how does that match up with my life?
- How well do I understand God's grace?
- How well do I know God?
- How well do I reflect God's Spirit in the fruit I produce through my words and actions?

Unlocking the mystery behind God's intentions for you isn't that hard, but it does take time. You have to build a relationship with God. You need to ask Him to help you understand your purpose, and then you need to listen. When you discover what He wants, you need to obey. That means surrendering your will to His; living your life for His purpose, not yours.

Surrendering to God means trusting fully that, no matter how difficult or painful, what He asks of you is *always* in your best interest. Living for God means choosing to dedicate your life to Him, seeking His will for you and then following it.

That's not easy. If you apply yourself to it, however, over time your understanding of *what* God wants will grow. Your spiritual maturity will grow. Your *desire* to obey Him will grow.

There is purpose in everything God does, and His purpose is the only path that will lead you to ultimate happiness (Romans 8:28). If you make your whole life about growing in the grace and knowledge of Him and His Word, about serving others rather than yourself—then you *will* be living His divine purpose for you, every day.

Connecting Purpose to Roles

Once you understand God's divine purpose for you, then you can truly understand your roles and how to function within them. God's purpose helps give your roles meaning.

- What is my role as a godly woman?
- What is my role as a wife and mother?
- What is my role as a single woman?
- What is my role as a professional?
- How am I using those roles to best fulfill God's purpose for me?

Not all roles will live up to your expectations. You must take some responsibility for that, because God doesn't micromanage your life. Instead, take an honest look at what you have, where you are, and how well you are using that to be the woman God wants you to be.

Using Your God-Given Gifts

Another aspect to consider is that each of us has been given a unique set of talents, gifts, and abilities. Some were inherited and some developed through years of practice. Some may be obvious: musical ability, athletic prowess, artistic creativity. Other gifts may be less obvious, but no less important.

For example, you may be a great encourager or listener. You may be great at hosting and entertaining. You may have exceptionally good analytical or organizational skills.

As Christian women we need to ask ourselves:

- Do I know what my gifts and abilities are?
- Do I have gifts and abilities that I am not focusing on?

- Am I using them to fulfill God's purpose for me, no matter what my roles?
- Am I using them to serve others, not just myself?

I have the gift of listening to people and being intuitive. I have become a good public speaker, an effective teacher, and a decent writer. I use those abilities and gifts in my various roles: counselor, coach, author, and mentor, to name a few. Don't waste time comparing your gifts with others' and then feel inadequate (or arrogant if you are especially gifted). Instead, focus on the fact that they were God-given to *assist* you in living out your purpose.

Changing Perspective

Don't get hung up on the wrong things. Each of us has been through life experiences that have shaped the person we are now. Some of those experiences have been traumatic or challenging. A life that's being lived out of disappointment or regret is not an intentional one.

If you want to be more intentional about life but you're feeling stuck, look beyond this life. If you don't, things start to look bleak and it's easy to lose perspective (1 Corinthians 15:19). Perspective—our mental outlook on life—has a huge impact on how we live. Your perspective is your reality.

Sometimes we have to change spaces to change perspective. Have you ever asked yourself how God sees your situation? What would it be like to view your life from where He is? I mean, literally. Imagine sitting where He is, on His throne, and looking down at you, one person on a planet of over seven billion people.

He has a much different perspective. After all, He has the biggest picture. He knows how your situation fits into the overall scheme of life. He hasn't forgotten you. He hasn't dropped the ball. If you trust Him, then you can trust His perspective.

Stepping into His perspective is difficult, however, when you aren't close to Him. When you begin to question *why* you're dealing with certain things, and *how* you're going to handle them, and wonder *when* they'll be over, you aren't looking at things from His point of view.

You're looking at it from your own, and that's a dangerous thing to do.

When life's stressors are viewed only from the perspective of how they impact you, negativity can set in. Negative thoughts and emotions cause us to behave in ways that are hurtful to ourselves and others. They keep us stuck.

They cause us to react out of our emotions: confusion, fear, hurt, and anger. We say things we can't take back. We pull within to protect ourselves. We avoid dealing with people and situations that may cause us further hurt instead of working through them to find resolution. We become anxious, expecting the worst.

We think only of ourselves.

It's not always possible to understand things. We can't fully know why people say or do things, why we go through certain situations, or why life hasn't turned out the way we wanted.

Coming to terms with not having children was a process for me. But through it all I never put my life on hold, because I didn't make it my purpose, my reason for living. I was absolutely determined to keep living my life. Did I struggle with the *why*? Absolutely. Looking back, I can see how God gave me many opportunities to nurture and care for other people's children, both as a therapist, and by being the very best aunt I could be to my nieces and nephews.

Life is hard. If you want to change it, *and you can*, then

your perspective must shift. Change can't happen until it does (Psalm 40:1–3).

WORKBOOK

Chapter Four Questions

Question: What (or whom) are you letting define you that's keeping you from being intentional? What conduct, life experiences, and internal beliefs more correctly define who you are?

_____
_____
_____
_____
_____
_____
_____
_____
_____
_____
_____

Question: List your current roles, as well as your gifts and abilities.

Question: In what ways have you confused your roles with your purpose? How are they different?

Question: What would you say is your "end goal" in life? How does this translate into your purpose? How can you keep an eternal perspective even when you are bogged down in the day-to-day of life?

_____
_____
_____
_____
_____
_____
_____
_____
_____

Action: Looking back over the things you have learned in this chapter, write out a purpose statement for your life.

_____
_____
_____
_____
_____

Chapter Four Notes

CHAPTER FIVE

Time to Dream

I'm a daydreamer. I'm also an idealist. I love to imagine life's possibilities, plan out the future in my head, and imagine myself already there. It's fun, but it's also beneficial to me. There was a time, though, when life seemed so hard. My dreams felt very much out of reach—not even worth pursuing. It didn't start that way.

When I finished graduate school at the age of 25, I knew exactly what I wanted, personally and professionally. However, life has a way of twisting and turning, taking you in directions you didn't anticipate. That was certainly true for me. I'd imagined myself in a private counseling practice for years, and when I finally realized that dream, it was exciting.

I knew I wanted to write. That was an ability I'd been gifted with, and one of my dreams had always been to write a book. I also wanted to find a way to encapsulate all the tools I'd given clients over the years. I formed a company with my sister that would market biblically-based educational courses and programs. We hired a website developer and I determined to write my first course on anger management, which I believed I could easily market given the demand I was seeing.

It was quite the process though: the development and writing of the program, the instructional design, recording each segment and then producing it into audio CDs and a workbook. When it was finally done, it was amazing to see the finished product and see the fruits of all our hard work—a dream finally realized.

A Change of Plans

Then something happened. I attended a workshop for continuing education credits and the keynote speaker kept talking about using horses with her clients. I'd never heard of such a thing, so I spoke with her afterwards about it. Later, knowing my husband would be interested, I mentioned it to him as well. He'd grown up around horses, unlike me, and had always wanted to find a way to own them again. The idea of incorporating his love and knowledge of horses with my counseling background was very intriguing to him.

That was the beginning of a new dream—but not one that belonged to me. Over the course of the next eight years, several decisions were made that changed the practice from what I'd intended it to be, to an equine-based therapy facility. We completed our certification, bought a couple of horses, and purchased 44 acres just 12 miles west of Riverton, Wyoming. We sold our home and built a 6,000-square-foot indoor arena, with offices at one end and living quarters directly above. My husband quit his full-time contracting business to run our hobby horse ranch and be my "horse specialist" in equine sessions with clients.

The company I'd started with my sister came to an end. There was no time to devote to it anymore. I had the one program we'd finished, but no time to market it. I sold the occasional copy to clients, and we paid for one advertisement in a Christian magazine, but that was all. The dream didn't go away. I just didn't have time to attend to it anymore. I was too busy making my husband's dream come true—and I did, for a while.

Two horses grew into a herd of seven. Our business grew from just the two of us to a part-time staff of eight. Our day would start around 6 a.m., with clients coming through the gates by 7:45 a.m. and often not leaving until 8:30 p.m. or later. Though I was grateful for the growing number of clients, I also felt an unanticipated level of stress with each car that drove up to the building.

Many times I would have to rush downstairs to open up the office lobby because a client had arrived early, and no other staff were there. Then I would go upstairs to finish getting ready. We worked hard to maintain boundaries between our home upstairs and the offices below, but it was challenging. Our workspace was so close, with clients coming and going all day long, that it became difficult to relax even after the last client had gone home.

Even after clients had left, my husband still had the horses to put away and feed and the arena to clean up. In the spring and summer months, there were also hay crops to irrigate each night. That meant dragging sprinkler pods around the fields—a labor-intensive process. Dinner was rarely on the table before 9 p.m. Sometimes I would go back down to my office after dinner to do paperwork that I hadn't had the chance to do earlier.

It was a never-ending cycle. Still, our client base grew as word in our community grew about this new, very effective type of therapy. We had constant referrals, began billing Medicaid and insurance, which increased both our workload and our income. It also increased our stress levels.

For starters, I was working with a lot of children—a natural byproduct of using horses. And while the equine-based approach worked, I personally did not enjoy working with children the way I did with adults. Yet I didn't feel that I had a choice. What we had chosen to do was expensive. We'd sunk a lot of money into the land and the building, along with all the start-up costs of a new business. Horses are not cheap, as anyone who owns one can tell you! So, I felt obligated to see whatever clients came our way, even if I didn't always enjoy what I was doing or who I was working with.

As the pressure to make more money grew—so that we could pay for the ranch and make payroll each month—so did the strain on our marriage. In addition, counseling wasn't as rewarding for my husband as he thought it would be. It turned out that he didn't like working with people who had so many challenges. He'd come from a business where he could see the tangible result of his efforts each day to something that was far more uncertain.

Additionally, he didn't like feeling like he was working for me. Yet the reality was that I was ultimately responsible for each client's progress. I was the only one who knew each person's full history due to confidentiality requirements. I was the one who knew the treatment plan and it was my licensure that was on the line if something happened.

We were partners, yet I felt a huge burden of responsibility. It began to affect my own mental health. I struggled to sleep at night, worrying about clients, money, billing, and employee issues. Occasionally I would think about my original plan, the programs I'd wanted to write. That dream seemed far away. Life was just too busy. So I stopped dreaming about it, and that changed me.

Instead of being excited and hopeful about the future, I became anxious and irritable. I was working long hours. There was rarely time to relax and enjoy our ranch, due to the reality of working and living out of the same space. That meant that we often wanted to get away from the ranch to enjoy down time, but with animals that needed to be tended to, that always presented a challenge for us.

Over time I came to see the ranch as a huge financial burden, out of which I saw no end. I felt angry and resentful, without fully understanding why.

Then other things began to happen. Medicaid slashed its reimbursement rates, making it cost-prohibitive for us to offer equine-based services to those clients. Given this, and the challenging nature of problems that we often encountered with Medicaid clients, dropping Medicaid seemed the right thing to do. However, it affected our client numbers considerably. That meant, of course, that we had to let some staff go.

That led to the ultimate decision to stop billing insurance altogether. Up until that point, we'd been running our practice like so many other health care practices: collecting co-pays and waiting for insurance payments, while providing weeks of service in the meantime. Though convenient for clients, it often meant chasing after money when insurance companies didn't pay, or only paid partial amounts. I began to ask myself, *"Why are we doing all this work and hoping to eventually get paid?"* It seemed like a foolish business model. I determined to make changes. Once again, however, the decision to stop billing insurance had a dramatic negative impact on our business and finances.

Looking back, I think I was subconsciously working my way back to my original dream, but in a very passive-aggressive way, regrettably. I hadn't come to terms with why I was unhappy, I just knew I was. I knew I needed to make changes and thought that if we changed the type of clients we saw, that would help.

Time to Change

In a way, it did.
We hired a business coach. After all, if I was still going

to see clients, I had to come up with a completely different approach, an "outside of the box" way of thinking and delivering services.

The timing was wrong. I was burned out. I'd been responsible for so much more than just my clients. I'd taken on the mental and emotional strain of trying to fix things that were crumbling before us—things that we'd both worked so hard to build. I found myself trying to control situations I really had no control over and the burden of it became too much.

At the end of 2012, I announced that I would retire from mental health by the end of the following year. I'm not sure what I actually thought I'd accomplish at the time. I just knew that I'd run out of energy, and passion, for what we were doing. Then, two weeks after my announcement, my back started hurting.

My fears intensified. You would think I'd be relieved to walk away from something that had created so much stress. Instead I found myself terrified of how we were going to financially survive. I'd come to believe, for many reasons, that I was the primary provider for our family. Now what?

I still had a handful of clients. Armed with some ideas from the business coach, I began implementing some new strategies, marketing packages of services to clients instead of having them pay session-by-session. I offered them introductory pricing and it worked. More clients.

Still, it wasn't enough. My back pain was getting increasingly worse, making it difficult for me to sit more than two hours at a time. I tried physical therapy. Unfortunately, I'd already dropped our health insurance to save costs, so I could only afford so much.

Things seemed increasingly hopeless. We were using up our savings each month, supplementing the meager earnings I was bringing in with my small handful of clients, and a few horseback riding clients my husband had.

By 2013, we'd stopped virtually all equine services for our clients. I was back to seeing them in the office and my husband was primarily teaching horsemanship skills to a handful of children.

It wasn't enough to pay for the costs of the ranch and I was painfully aware of that. By this time, I'd begun exploring the idea of getting my coaching certification and took a couple of online classes with that in mind. One class spurred an idea that blossomed into a course of my own. For the first time in ages, I felt energy again as I began developing and writing the course. I marketed it to some former clients as an interactive program to be offered via teleconference, and a handful of women signed up. I was on my way!

About two-thirds of the way through the course, I had to finally acknowledge that my back was too bad. I just couldn't sit long enough to write, let alone deliver each lesson plan. I informed the women that I was having to end the program prematurely, and that was that.

I hit an all-time low. I didn't know what else to do for my back. Our financial situation seemed dire, but I didn't know how to resolve it. I began having panic attacks.

Then my parents came to visit us. They could see that we were struggling and before they left, they pulled me aside one day and handed me an envelope with 1000 dollars. "Go get help for your back," they said.

So, I did. And for the first time in months I felt hope. That money became the catalyst that moved me back towards my dream, though it would be several more years before I was fully back on track again. More about that later.

Why Dream?

What about you? Do you dream anymore? I bet that once upon a time you had all kinds of wonderful dreams just waiting to burst out of you and become reality. A dream, at its core, is a mental image or succession of images. Those images may be very tentative or incredibly defined. They may contain bodily sensations and provoke certain emotions. They may occur subconsciously (while you sleep), pop into your head when you least expect them, or be part of a concerted, conscious effort. In all instances, dreams involve *imagination*. The imagery contained within your dreams is extremely useful because, as you sift and sort through them, you can begin to form a *blueprint* for life.

The most useful type of dreaming is self-directed. Dreams that occur at night are your brain's way of sifting and sorting through the day's events—processing information, sensations, emotions, and experiences. Dreams, however, that guide you towards living intentionally require conscious effort on your part. Self-directed dreams give you something to look forward to, to strive toward. They also give you opportunity to be creative.

Your brain needs time to creatively process, *imagine* possibilities, and arrive at solutions.

When we dream, we are testing out possibilities *before they happen*. The use of *inductive* and *deductive* reasoning, formulating original ideas, and using critical thought—all of these are sophisticated abilities that are relied upon when you dream *with intention*. That's healthy for your brain. Complex thinking allows you to understand new ideas, connect the dots, read between the lines, and take calculated risks. And the best news—dreaming is a great way to *improve* your complex thinking skills!

So when you dream—about relationships, the home you want to have, the children you want to raise, the places you want to explore, the career you want to build—you are designing that life blueprint.

Dreaming teaches you a few things too—about

yourself! Your dreams are the lifeblood of *who you are*. They reveal what excites you, makes you come alive, and fills you with passion, energy, joy. They are a synthesis of who you've been, who you are now, and who you're desiring to be. The more you dream about something, the more you *practice* that dream in your mind. As the saying goes, "Practice makes perfect." I think a better way to say it, however, is like this: "Mental practice makes purposeful productivity." The more you think about what you want, the more likely you are to move yourself in that direction.

Where are your dreams taking you?

It's not enough to have a dream. Your dream must *take you somewhere.* That's the difference between being a dreamer and a visionary. A dreamer *imagines* how her life could be. A visionary *sees* how her life could be, then sets out to make it happen. A vision for your life means thinking about the future: what you want, what God wants for you, and *why*, rather than just drifting from one situation to another. It means planning, with foresight and wisdom. It means considering the consequences of your intentions *before* you act on them.

Having vision:

- Creates passion and inspiration
- Provides a target on which to focus resources and energy
- Allows you to plan with intention
- Motivates against challenges, setbacks, emotional and financial hardships
- Prevents you from making foolish errors with lifelong consequences

A vision is not a dream but a reality that hasn't happened yet. There are four components to having vision:

1. Purpose

As I covered in a previous chapter, this is your *why*—the reason you're doing what you're doing. Who benefits and how? Having purpose for your dream is how you find the motivation to stick it out when you encounter setbacks.

The "right" purpose helps. My overall purpose has always been to strive to live a godly life, based on God's Word, to seek first His Kingdom and His righteousness (Matthew 6:33). I've tried to fit my dreams and goals into that context, which is why I set out to take my professional experiences and turn them into biblically-based content for Christian women. I didn't have a clear vision, however, of how I intended to do that. I implemented an idea, without knowing fully where I wanted it to take me.

And as a result, I allowed myself to be pulled off course.

2. Clarity

Vision, by its very definition, needs to be clear and well-defined. What should you do with those dreams? Write them down! There's nothing worse than a dream that floats into your consciousness, only to disappear just as quickly—*and you didn't grab it before it was gone.* I've been frustrated on multiple occasions when I wished, futilely, that I could recall that "great idea" I'd had. Now I find a way to capture those random thoughts—a notebook, my phone, a voice recorder.

Not all dreams occur randomly though. Setting aside time to *purposefully* dream is essential to creating an intentional life. Your dreams are your starting point because

they provide energy, excitement and movement to your day. Without them, life becomes drudgery.
   You do that by starting at the end and working backwards. In other words, what's your destination? What do you want to achieve and *why*? What will life look like once you've achieved it? What will *you* look like? Will your roles have changed? Will your relationships be different? Will the physical space around you change?

   One of my clients, Susan, felt stuck in her life because her home was filled with unnecessary clutter. When she *wove* the de-cluttering of each room into her dreams her ability to envision a more intentional future became possible. It was as though each room represented an aspect of the life she wanted to create. An organized kitchen helped her define the family bond she wanted to establish with her children. A tidy bedroom led to improved communication and intimacy with her husband. The spare bedroom became her personal office space and occasional gym, leading to increased productivity and greater wellbeing. It took her time, however, to really understand the connection between her physical environment and what she was wanting to change.
   I've come to realize that I too need to give myself time to define my dreams. Sometimes I get excited about ideas and begin carrying them out before I've really thought them through. Often those ideas cost me time, energy and even money. They can be expensive! How many times have I paid for a new website before I've completely thought through the content I want, only to have to pay for it to be redone? How many purchases have I made for office equipment that turned out to not be necessary? How many workshops have I signed up for, only to not need the information because my dreams took me down a different path, once they were fully defined?
   Too many times!

Dreaming is fun, or it ought to be. It's fun because when you dream, the sky's the limit—or beyond! You don't let yourself be hampered by lack of money, lack of support, lack of time, lack of energy. You just dream! When you do, when you just free up your brain to let loose, something fantastic happens. Your brain starts to relax. It starts to move into creative mode. One dream flows into another, and another, and another.

3. Values

Values are those deeply held beliefs or principles that guide your decision-making. They are expressed both internally, in the way you think and perceive things, and externally, through your behaviors. Some values lead to positive outcomes, some to negative ones. In order to live *authentically* and *intentionally*, you must **live** your values. If you don't know what matters most to you, how can you have a clear vision of what you intend?

Your values are shaped by several factors: upbringing, knowledge, emotion, thought, and perception. How you determine them and how you live them is critical because they influence everything—the way you see the world and the way you respond to it. They are the basis for how you make ethical decisions. In turn, your individual values help to shape societal views. As the moral and ethical standards of a society change, so do the laws that govern it. Conversely, as societal values change so do individual ones, *if* you allow your individual values to be shaped by societal pressure and public opinion.

Sometimes our values are *right*, but the choices we're making aren't leading us to them. If that's the case it may be time to step back and ask yourself some important questions:

- How do I determine the right values from the

wrong ones?
- If I don't have the right values, what will happen?
- Is it enough to just trust whether those values feel right or wrong?
- How do I know when I need to step back and reevaluate whether my intentional choices are fundamentally sound?
- What do I do when I realize I've been living an intentional life based on the wrong values, or when my choices aren't leading me to the right ones?

A recent conversation with a client illustrates this. Jan has been pursuing money her whole career. Money represented stability and security. She grew up with poverty and it was a difficult life, so she determined that being wealthy would be her *primary* measure of success. She likened it to climbing a mountain. With each purposeful career decision she made, she climbed higher. Her responsibilities grew. Her salary grew. Now she's at the top of the mountain, but she's discovered that she doesn't like the view.

She climbed the wrong mountain.

Even though she was very *intentional* about it, Jan's goal of being wealthy didn't lead her to her core values of stability and security. Once she realized what her values are, she was able to identify what actions would actually help her *live* them. Though the money doesn't help her achieve some of her core values, it does give her the means to achieve other things she values: having the freedom to travel, pursue educational goals and spend time with family, amongst others.

If you are ambivalent about your values, then there's a greater chance that you will follow the mainstream in accepting what is or is not moral or ethical. This means, of course, that your thoughts and actions will also be dictated by mainstream opinion.

Are you okay with that?

I'm not. Few people actually *choose* their values, but if you want to live a divinely intentional life you must. You cannot simply adopt the values of others. That's because they may be carrying you down a path that's leading you away from where you truly want to go!

These days I've learned to pay attention to that uneasiness that I occasionally feel when what I'm doing isn't aligned with what I believe and value. That uneasiness tells me that I need to take a hard look at my actions. Do they match up with what I profess to live by?

That doesn't mean that I always live my values. No one does. There have been a number of times when fear of the unknown, or fear of all the worst possibilities, has pulled me away from my core values and led me back to the *familiar* path.

That's because we sometimes base our decisions on emotions, not values. We convince ourselves of the "rightness" of our choices because of how we're feeling. We think we're aligning our choices with our values. In reality, we're just being self-serving or emotionally reactive.

The year 2013 stands out as one of those times for me, in glaring neon lights. So many decisions I made that year weren't based on what really mattered to me, but out of fear and uncertainty.

By the middle of that year, just contemplating the future was exhausting. I was so burned out with the day-to-day that stringing more than two tasks together felt like hard work. I was in a mental fog, with no light at the end of the proverbial tunnel. When you're that stressed, moving forward *intentionally* seems like a monumental, exhausting task. Strong forces continually try to drag you backwards and down.

Then something changed—and hope came back. The money my parents gave me opened a door. Stepping through that door, exploring possible health solutions, put me back in charge of my life. I'd stopped believing I had any control over my back pain; that I had to just find a way to live with it. Now, for the first time in months, I felt like I had *permission* to hope again.

It wasn't until I began being proactive about my health that I began to slowly find my way back to my original dreams. Taking charge of something I could control was a catalyst for helping me to get intentional about other aspects of my life again. Once again I found myself dreaming.

That's what dreams do for you; they give you hope.

4. Goals

How do you turn your vision into *intentional* actions? You set goals. Somewhere in your past you've probably *wished* something into being. You thought about it so much, fleshed it out in such vivid, kaleidoscopic color, that it began to change the way you thought and *behaved*. Those changed behaviors led to your dream being realized.

The clearer your vision is, the easier it is to determine what steps you need to take. Your goals are the mile markers that lead to your destination. Once you've identified them you can move forward with *intention*. However, you can't set goals until you've defined your vision. Having an *idea* of where you want to go, who you want to be, is not enough.

Goals take you beyond an idea—they are the "how to" for implementing your vision. More about that in the next chapter.

For now, consider this.

Each of us dreams in one way or another about something—or we used to. Do those dreams seem like a hazy, distant memory now? Do you even recall your dreams?

If that's true, what happened?

Maybe there have been too many disappointments along the way; too many people have let you down. You let yourself down. Things didn't turn out the way you expected.

It's true. Often the reality of what we've been dreaming about is different than the expectation. Our marriage is harder than we anticipated, our children have minds of their own, opportunities don't always come knocking when we want them to, and sometimes we make stupid mistakes that mess up these opportunities. People hurt us, and we hurt them back. It's easier to stop dreaming. That way you don't get hurt again.

Wrong!

I'd spent my entire life dreaming about what I wanted, and then I allowed myself to get derailed. That's not anyone's fault but mine. I determined to put my husband's dream first and I thought that I could incorporate our two dreams together. What happened, instead, is that I gave up all the things I'd wanted, that I knew I was good at, to do something I didn't know how to do and wasn't passionate about. And we both paid a price.

There are dreams you still have, that are just waiting to be realized. Aligning those dreams with what God intends for you is what being *divinely intentional* is about. When life gets challenging and overwhelming, *imagining* a better life can feel self-indulgent and wasteful. In those times, it may feel like you're in survival mode. No mental time to waste. If you've stopped dreaming, you've stopped thinking about what makes you happy. You've stopped learning about yourself.

WORKBOOK

Chapter Five Questions

Question: What dreams fueled you when you were younger? Do you still have the same dreams?

_____
_____
_____
_____
_____
_____
_____
_____
_____
_____
_____

Question: How have your dreams changed over the years? Are there areas where you have stopped dreaming because of disappointment or fear?

_____
_____
_____
_____
_____
_____
_____
_____
_____
_____

Question: What are your core values and are your dreams aligned with them or not?

_____
_____
_____
_____
_____
_____

_____

_____

_____

_____

_____

Question: How clearly do you see your future, even beyond this life? What can you do to make it even clearer?

_____

_____

_____

_____

_____

_____

_____

_____

_____

_____

_____

Action: Considering the four components of a vision (purpose, clarity, values, and goals), write down your thoughts (single words or phrases) that will help you begin to define a vision plan for the intentional life you want to build. Start with your purpose—the *why*—then jot down anything you want to change about yourself and the life you currently have. Don't limit yourself, just dream!

_____
_____
_____
_____
_____
_____
_____
_____
_____
_____
_____

Chapter Five Notes

CHAPTER SIX

The Pyramid Perspective

Life is about relationships. A *balanced* life is one that is all about *balanced* relationships. That means you have to prioritize them so that they reflect what's most important to you. An *intentional* life is about making choices that *reveal* to others just what those priorities are.

Relationships are essential to our well-being in so many ways (I know I've said this already, but it's worth repeating). They keep us connected, give us support, and ideally, they help us keep a healthy perspective. However, not all relationships are equal.

Think of a pyramid. The top of the pyramid is your most important relationship, then the next, then the next, and so on. The time you invest in each relationship needs to be prioritized accordingly.

Sometimes we may say some relationships are more important, when in reality we behave as though there are no perceptible differences. That would be like viewing our relationships on a continuum. Everyone who is vying for our attention gets it on a first-come-first-served basis.

Living this way leads to imbalance, stress, and ultimately, unhappiness.

Viewing your relationships as a pyramid helps you to evaluate just who *ought* to be getting the best of you, and whether your choices truly are reflecting that. Since God is the only true source for figuring out your life purpose, He needs to be at the top of your relationship pyramid. Only God can secure your ultimate future, the one beyond this lifetime.

It's true though, that while some relationships aren't as important to you, they might take up more time. For example, if you work outside of the home, your job gets a huge chunk of your day. If you are parenting infants or toddlers, your days and nights are consumed with their needs. It's easy to drop time with God when we're trying to attend to others. It's also easy to stop attending to ourselves. Others' needs may feel more important.

Imagine that you're a pitcher of water, and every relationship that you have is represented by an empty glass, clamoring to be filled. That's what you do. You fill others up. But what happens when you run dry?

Do you still try to fill others up, knowing that you don't have anything left to give? Do you blame others for your emptiness? Do you blame your husband, your children, your job? Whose responsibility is it to keep you filled up so that you can continue to serve others?

Imbalance leads to burnout.

Women are nurturers by nature, but we aren't always good at realizing the value of nurturing ourselves. We're juggling so many roles and responsibilities these days careers, marriage, motherhood, overseeing the home, even responsibilities for elderly parents.

Caring for others can be both rewarding and exhausting. Over time, though, it can drain you of energy—mentally, emotionally, and physically. It becomes necessary, then, to replenish yourself. After all, if you're not healthy then how can you give your best to others? How can you model healthy behaviors?

That's why the second most important relationship in that pyramid is with yourself.

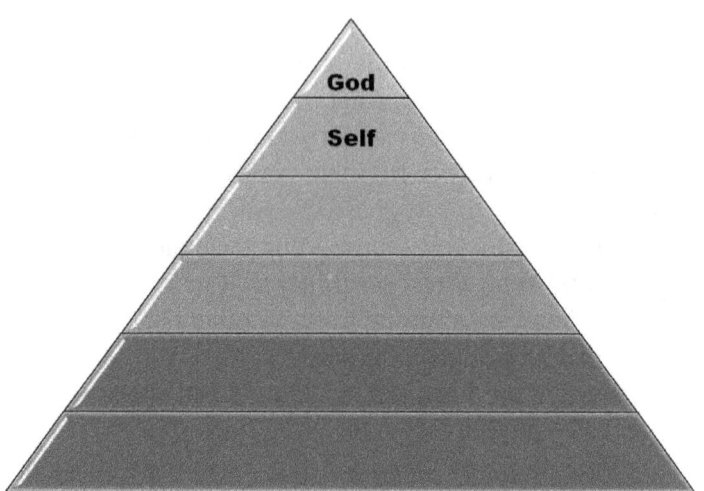

Taking care of yourself is not a job for others and it can't be something you fit into the crevices of your day. If that's what you're doing, then what's already begun to happen? Are you feeling burned out? Exhausted? Overwhelmed? Irritable? Discouraged? Numb? Are you just living on autopilot, getting through the busyness of the day, your wheels spinning but not gaining much traction?

That's what happened to me. The pressure of running a business, running a home, meeting client needs, employee needs, my husband's needs—it was too much. There didn't seem to be time for me to think about my own wellbeing. I was too exhausted, and too afraid of what would happen if I dropped any of my responsibilities.

It became a rut that my husband and I both fell into without realizing it. After you do something over and over for a period of time, it just becomes habit. If what you're habitually doing is not intentionally moving you towards the life you want to create, your brain, body, sense of self and family will eventually take a dive.

Being balanced, then, also represents the relationship

between taking care of you versus taking care of everybody else.

The Inverted Pyramid

Sometimes we give lip service to the idea of prioritizing our relationships, but our actions say otherwise. We invert our pyramid.

The inverted pyramid is a pyramid turned upside-down. Instead of spending time with God and yourself first so that you can be your healthiest, you give to everyone else first. A typical inverted pyramid might look like this:

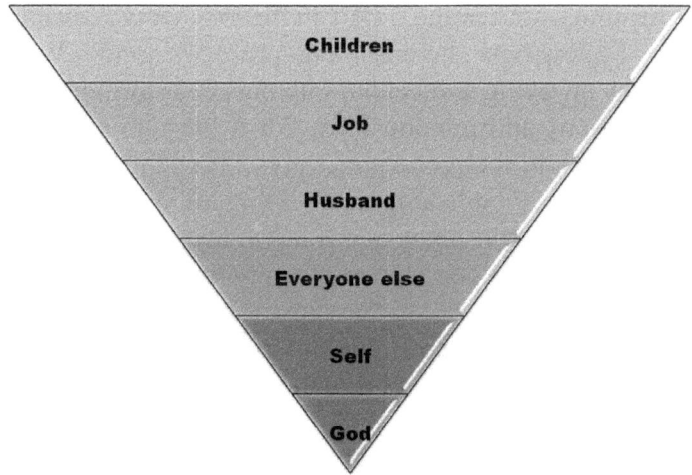

Sometimes we invert our pyramid because we're looking for validation in the wrong places.

When we connect our self-worth to what others think of us, we are setting ourselves up for hurt. People will ultimately let us down, disappoint, or betray us. Perhaps not intentionally, but it will happen. If your self-worth is tied up in pleasing others, then it will fluctuate based on how happy *they are*. On the other hand, self-worth that comes from God—from knowing how much He loves and cares for you and has a plan *for* you—isn't subject to others' opinions.

Samantha is a single woman in her twenties who struggles with an inverted pyramid, like so many of us. "Sometimes I feel like being balanced is about being perfect," she shared with me, as though she has to be able to do it all and do it well. The problem is, she struggles with thinking her self-worth is connected to what she accomplishes. She also has a hard time communicating her needs. "I'm too self-reliant," she admits. Being able to ask for alone time is hard, though she recognizes that it's healthier for her and others in the long run.

I know how she feels. You probably do too. We often grow up trying to meet our internal needs through external situations and relationships. For a long time, I believed that I could feel good about myself as long as I was producing, accomplishing and helping. While I was helping others, I wasn't being very kind to myself.

Even when you realize it's important to prioritize relationships, it can be challenging to strike a healthy balance. How much time do I give to God? How much time do I give myself? How do I *find* the time to do both?

There's no perfect answer. I can only say that when I determined that I needed to make some serious changes, I found the time. I stopped worrying about *how* and I just determined to *do* what needed to be done. Here's what I discovered:

When your relationships are prioritized correctly, everything flows down from there. If your relationship with God is at the top of your pyramid, then His influence ripples out and touches all your other relationships in a positive way.

Knowing that you matter to God helps you to realize

that you must take care of yourself, and treat yourself with respect, honor, and love. The Bible tells us to love others as we love ourselves (Matthew 22:39). If you don't love yourself, in a healthy, non-narcissistic way, then how do you know how to outwardly express that love to others?

That's why self-care is not selfish; it's *selfless*. It's selfless because your loved ones need to see you valuing and taking care of yourself for *their* sake, not just your own.

Part of self-care has to do with how you let others treat you.

- Do you let them walk all over you?
- Do you let them take advantage of you?
- Do you let them abuse your time?
- Do you let them abuse you mentally, emotionally, or even physically?
- Do you have healthy boundaries in your relationships?
- Can you say no to people?

We teach others how to treat us. That's why it's so important that you believe in the necessity of what you're doing. If you doubt yourself, if you believe that it's selfish to take care of yourself first, that doubt will be conveyed to others when you ask for support. It will make you second guess yourself and you'll be more likely to cave when others pressure you to return to the status quo.

The Four Areas of Self-Care

What *is* self-care?

Self-care is about being holistically healthy. It's about recognizing the connectedness between mind, body and spirit. When one is weak, the others are negatively impacted. Self-care, then, is preventive medicine.

In other words, self-care is an intentional and powerful choice to be your healthiest—spiritually, mentally, emotionally and physically. After all, you aren't really healthy unless you're healthy all over.

The most important aspect of your overall well-being is your **spiritual health**. When God is first, everything else in your life improves. Part of your self-care then, is taking time out to be with God, and reflecting on the deeper, weightier matters of life, like:

- Do I have purpose for living?
- Are the choices I make each day moving me towards that purpose?
- Do I believe in God and have a close, intimate friendship with Him?
- Do I spend time with encouraging, inspiring people who believe as I do, and who remind me of my purpose in life?

Your **mental health** has to do with what you think, how you perceive the world around you, the meaning you attach to situations and your attitude in general. If your primary focus is negative, towards yourself and/or others, then it can be said that your mental health is poor, which makes you susceptible to emotionally-based illnesses and other diseases.

Your mental health is, of course, affected by your spiritual health. If you don't have any hope for a future beyond this life—if you have no purpose or meaning for your existence—then what's the point?

Being mentally healthy also means keeping your mind sharp and active. Consider the following:

- Do I engage in activities that keep my brain sharp and active?
- Do I manage my thoughts so that they reflect and support positive, encouraging outcomes?
- Do I deal with negative situations and people and then move on, without letting them hold me down?
- Am I careful to protect my mind from dangerous or damaging information, situations or material?

Your **emotional health** is closely connected to your mental health because you *feel* based on how you think. Negative thoughts breed negative emotions. Positive thoughts breed positive emotions. Sounds simple perhaps, and in theory it is. The reality of managing your thoughts so that you can control your feelings is a difficult, ongoing process. Sometimes we can get stuck in deep ruts of our own making, however, because we only see a situation from one perspective. Talking out our situation with someone else—a friend, a relative, a minister, a therapist or coach—might be necessary for climbing out of that hole we've dug ourselves into.

Consider these questions as you evaluate just how emotionally healthy you are:

- Do I keep my emotions in control, instead of letting them control me?
- Do I use my emotions as a guide to address areas of my life that need work?
- Am I able to identify root causes of damaging emotions, such as anger, resentment and bitterness, and deal with them decisively?

- Am I careful to nurture emotions that support my desire for a satisfying, purposeful life?

Finally, your **physical health** is about both your body and your environment. It's about respecting yourself, and those around you, to engage in safe practices, keep your home and surroundings free of clutter and create a space that is conducive for overall well-being.

Ask yourself:

- Do I engage in activities that keep my body active and healthy three to five times every week?
- Do I balance work with recreation, so that my mind and body have time to rest?
- Do I get enough quality sleep?
- Is my home a place that feels safe and relaxing? Is it clean and clutter free?
- Have I cultivated a network of supportive, loving relationships with others?
- Do I have a healthy, balanced approach to money and use it as a tool, rather than a way to fill a void in my life?

If your life is truly healthy and balanced, it will be reflected in your goals and supporting habits. Others will see and believe it by how you live your life.

For example, if you value having a relationship with God, those who spend time with you will see that in how you behave, the way you talk, the choices you make. In the same way, if family is important to you, then your goals will demonstrate that. If you value being professional, having integrity, making time for friends, it will show.

The way you prioritize and balance your relationships is completely connected to what you value. That's why it's critical to make sure that your dreams are based on what you value, because you're going to turn those dreams into goals, which are the milestones you set for yourself along the path to accomplishing your dreams. Without them your dreams won't be accomplished no matter how much you write them down.

What turns a dream into a goal is a five-step process called the SMART format. This acronym—generally attributed to George T. Doran, a consultant and former Director of Corporate Planning for the Washington Water Power Company[3]—stands for: Specific, Measurable, Attainable, Realistic and Time-oriented. When you take each of your dreams through this process, the finished product is a goal.

Even a goal won't be accomplished, however, without supporting habits.

Habits—and the mechanisms behind them—are very interesting, as Charles Duhigg addresses in his book *The Power of Habit*.[4] A habit is a consistently repeated behavior that forms over time. It starts with a conscious choice and eventually becomes something we do automatically. Good habits propel you forward, keep you motivated and help you see the results you're wanting. Bad habits can create mental and emotional atrophy. Your desire for something doesn't go away, but your ability to achieve it is dependent on those habits.

Living a Lie

The truth of that hit me squarely in 2013. I knew what I valued. I had tangible goals, but I wasn't living them. Instead I was going through the motions, yet mentally and emotionally exhausted and physically in pain.

I wanted life to be different. I could envision it, but my actual behaviors weren't supporting my vision. My behaviors had become habitual practices that were actually undermining my hope that anything would change.

I wanted my back pain to go away. By June of 2013, I'd been unable to exercise for about six months. Though I valued good health and a consistent exercise routine, I wasn't practicing it. Instead I was making excuses.

I'm a serious stickler for self-care these days, but there was a time when we were running our business that it seemed like a luxury I didn't have time for. We worked late because we had to provide evening hours. I'd be trying to make dinner at 8:30 p.m. yet still have paperwork to do. Then, we'd be up early the next morning to prepare for the first influx of clients. Life was an endless cycle of work and sleep, work and sleep, with the occasional vacation away if we could afford it and find animal care.

The money my parents gave me for my back was a game changer. It was the catalyst that set me back on the intentional living path. All of a sudden, I felt like I had options. I could begin exploring some solutions for my back pain. Chiropractic visits became part of my weekly routine. Then I began going to the community pool. At first all I did was put on a flotation belt and "jog" in the deep end. It didn't get my heart rate up, but it did do something unexpected. It gave me a mental and emotional respite from my stress. I found myself feeling less anxious, more hopeful.

Over time I began swimming laps instead. I gradually began increasing the number of laps I could do, and as I did, I felt my confidence begin to grow again. I was being proactive and creating new routines that were turning into positive habits. I also began to have ideas again, always an indication for me that I'm thinking about the future in a positive way.

One of those ideas led to my husband and I taking a real estate investment class. That led to us buying back our former home for less than we'd sold it for, renting out the living quarters of our ranch and lowering our monthly expenses.

My anxiety was diminishing, and I had greater hope for the future. Still, the idea of owning, marketing and running a business felt completely overwhelming. By late fall of 2013 I had only a small handful of clients. My husband had returned to construction out of necessity. We were getting ready to move off the ranch.

I realized something important. Though I'd intended to retire by the end of that year, I found that I really enjoyed working with the small number of private pay clients I still had. They were very invested in making changes and they demonstrated that through their financial commitment to the process. Therapy was fun and rewarding once again.

As 2014 emerged, life became a steady pattern of swimming, resting, seeing a few clients, taking care of the home, endless yard work, cooking meals, and studying real estate. Our newfound investment knowledge led to the acquisition of another property—a triplex. Then we converted our offices at the ranch into another apartment. Life seemed to be trending in a positive way again, or so I thought. I could see myself slowly inching back to a place of purpose and intention again. Old dreams were reawakening, bad habits were being identified.

It's What You Do That Matters

Seeing your life as a bunch of habits that need to be lit up, and then getting down to the hard work of changing what needs to be changed, is what intentional living is all about. The thing is, changing habits isn't necessarily easy, or quick. That's because we get into routines that become well-established. Those routines are made up of a series of behaviors that we follow over and over, until we no longer have to think about them. That's fine if it's something mindless, like tying your shoes. But you don't want your brain to disengage when it comes to important, life-altering choices.

The good news is that your habits are *not* your destiny! They're not in control. You are. They can be ignored, changed, or replaced.

Dream—Then Do

Let's tie this all together. You dream of a good life—a healthy, *balanced* life, with the people who matter most, right? So have you turned those dreams into tangible, measurable goals that have been broken down into smaller, daily steps that you can *intentionally* strive for and achieve? Are your habits going to move *you* toward those goals, or away from them? When there is a gap between what you want and what you have—or who you want to be versus who you currently are—it's probably because your habits are not supporting or setting you up for success.

So you are free to dream, and you *should,* but don't stop there.

WORKBOOK

Chapter Six Questions

Question: What does your relationship pyramid currently reflect in terms of how you prioritize and spend your time?

_____
_____
_____
_____
_____
_____
_____
_____
_____
_____

Question: Is your pyramid inverted?

Question: In what ways are your relationships lacking balance?

Question: Using the pitcher of water metaphor, whose responsibility is it to fill you up? How well is that happening?

_____
_____
_____
_____
_____
_____
_____
_____
_____
_____

Question: In which of the four areas of health is your self-care the strongest? In which area are you the weakest?

_____
_____
_____
_____
_____
_____

Action: Write out a self-care plan, identifying goals in all four areas of health. Transfer each goal to a 3x5 index card (preferably a different color for each of the four health areas).

_____

_____

_____

_____

_____

_____

_____

_____

_____

_____

Chapter Six Notes

CHAPTER SEVEN

A Sidetracked Dream

What good does it do you if you know where you're going, but you don't have a plan for how to get there? What if you have a plan but no way to actually implement it? What if the people in your life don't support your vision for the future? What if their desires take you in the completely opposite direction, or create difficult challenges for you?

I married three weeks after my twenty-sixth birthday to a man who is very different from me in education, in upbringing, in lifestyle, and in likes and dislikes.

He was fun, and he was well-liked by many. He was a hard worker, he was affectionate, and he liked to serve and help others—all admirable qualities that I definitely wanted in a man. The real clincher for me was that we both had the same spiritual values and goals.

When I met him, it was evident that he saw himself as a cowboy. He certainly dressed the part boots, Wranglers, hat, belt buckle—he had it all. He talked as though he'd grown up on a ranch and identified with that way of life. It was certainly a dream he had for his future, though I didn't realize that when I married him.

I, on the other hand, had very little experience with

horses, other than the occasional trail ride. Though I loved horses (from a distance), I feared them. They were big. They could kick and bite. I didn't relish the idea of falling off of one. Having horses and learning to be an expert rider were never parts of my dream for the future.

There were other differences, including the way we handled conflict and the way we made decisions. My husband didn't like conflict at all and went to great lengths to avoid it. He would agree with me just to avoid arguing, though I didn't realize this initially. I, on the other hand, saw conflict as part of any relationship—not always fun but usually unavoidable and often helpful.

When it came to making decisions, I was the "idea" person, so I was constantly coming up with plans for us. We would discuss them, weigh out the pros and cons, and invariably he would agree, or so it seemed.

As I look back, I realize now that in some ways I pursued my husband's dream, not just out of a desire to please him, but out of guilt. He'd supported my ideas for eleven years already. He'd moved away from his family to start a new life in Wyoming. He'd left behind all he'd known in 1997, gave up his job without having another, all so that I could take on a one-year position at a Community College in Wyoming. Neither of us knew what we'd do beyond that year, nor where we'd live. We both wanted to leave Texas, and the job seemed like our ticket out. It was.

My husband's decision to start his own construction and remodeling business when we first moved to Wyoming seemed like a good fit at the time. He is a very skilled carpenter. While he made it apparent that carpentry wasn't what he wanted to do for the rest of his life, it was a place to start.

However, as anyone who's owned their own business knows, there's far more to it than just being good at a skill or trade. Being a good carpenter did not mean that he knew how to run a business. Neither did I for that matter.

I knew nothing in the beginning about the infrastructure of a business—accounting, bookkeeping, taxes, billing, and marketing—but I was willing to learn. I had to.

In 2006 when we began to transition to our equine-based business, I was already tired. I'd been working a full-time job and doing the support work for his business for nine years. I'd hoped, in quitting my full-time job, that I would be able to pursue my professional dreams.

In truth, my husband's dream wasn't feasible without me. In fact, it wasn't really a dream, but more of a persona that'd he'd taken on. He saw himself as a cowboy, and all that was missing was the ranch and horses. My counseling license gave him the wherewithal to acquire both. My cashed-in retirement from the college I'd worked at provided us with the down payment for the ranch. My skill set gave us the ability to market a unique service. My acquired business knowledge kept us running.

That's not to say he did nothing. He became certified as an Equine Specialist. He took on the monumental project of general contracting the arena and our home. Once the metal structure was built, he almost singlehandedly built the framed two-story structure—within the metal framework of the arena—that would become our offices and living quarters. Though we had significant help from family for the initial build, it would be many years before it was all complete.

Through it all, he managed and took care of the horses, the land, the hay crops we grew, and all the equipment. None of that provided a living, but someone still had to do it. He was happy, for the most part. He was now living his dream. He had his ranch and he had the lifestyle he'd always wanted. He owned horses. There was just one huge problem.

I wasn't happy. I was exhausted. I'd walked away from my own dream and submersed myself in his.

Have you ever done that?

Have you ever gotten caught up in someone else's dream and lost sight of your own? It's so easy to fall into situations that pull you away from your dreams.

I see women all the time who *fall* into relationships. They *fall* into jobs or unexpected careers. They *fall* into circumstances without knowing how or why. Difficult circumstances, painful circumstances. They feel powerless to do anything about it.

Life just seems to have crept up on them without warning, stealing all the dreams they were once passionate about.

Perhaps they feel that it's too late; that it's impossible to change, or too hard, or too expensive. Perhaps they're fearful of what change will bring, so they settle for just meandering along life's path, being pulled in various directions by forces they can't (or won't) control.

The thing is, you can and should pursue your dreams, as long as they're within the framework of what God wants and expects from you. While it's not wrong to support someone else's dreams, if you subjugate your own dreams in the process, it will only lead to burnout and unhappiness.

Giving up your own dreams to make someone else happy *is not balanced.* It's not sustainable.

I love the example of the Proverbs 31 woman. Though some may see her as an impossible ideal, I don't at all. Instead, I look at her as a wonderful description of a woman who has *determined* who she wants and needs to be.

As you read through her description in Proverbs 31, you get the image of a very capable woman. She's a wife and mother, a businesswoman, an entrepreneur. She knows how to utilize the gifts and abilities God gave her to be a help to her husband and her children, to produce merchandise, to organize a busy household. Her husband values and supports her. While she undoubtedly looks up to and respects him—follows his leadership—she is still a woman with her own unique interests and talents, which she uses to her family's benefit (Proverbs 31:10–31). She doesn't serve herself; she serves her loved ones. She is not living in her husband's shadow.

How are you cultivating your own God-given talents and abilities? Have you lost sight of your own dreams to make someone else happy? Are you pursuing the desires of others at the expense of your own? Many women I work with are not self-aware enough to even see this as a problem. They believe they should submit at all costs.

Submission is a choice. It does not mean losing your identity or giving up on your own dreams. Submission doesn't equal submersion.

To be fair, my husband did not ask me to give up my dream for him. I did that on my own. I didn't spend any time analyzing it. It just happened. More and more time was devoted to the equine side of the business, leaving less time for writing. It was a slow, gradual drift away from what I'd intended, until one day, I wasn't devoting any time to it at all. There was no time left to give.

I'd never wanted the private practice to be our sole income, because I didn't want that pressure. But as it grew, it became necessary for my husband to become full-time as well. So he "retired" his tool belt in 2008. The pressure to grow was increasing.

As the years passed, I became angry, resentful, depressed, and anxious. There were never enough hours in the day for either of us. While he was doing things he loved—training his horses and caring for the ranch—I was stuck inside my office handling the mundane tasks that had to be done. I'd asked him countless times to help with bookkeeping, but it required computer skills he didn't have.

There's a difference between a balloon floating in the sky, and a balloon tethered to the ground. The tethered balloon is still airborne, floating freely, but it's also grounded in reality. By late 2013, I was dealing with the reality that my husband's dream had changed me in unforeseen ways. It was a dream I felt I could no longer sustain for him. I would have to cut it loose and let it fly away.

I was in constant pain yet trying to keep up appearances and keep everything running the best I could. I grasped at any income opportunities I could find, while begging my husband to return to carpentry. By this time, we weren't offering much equine counseling. I was back to seeing clients in my office. He was teaching horsemanship to a small handful of children and took in the occasional horse to be trained. Neither of us was bringing in enough income to sustain the costs of the ranch, so every month I would drain our savings a little more.

This was when the panic attacks began. It wasn't until I finally surrendered my fears to God that things began to change. I quit trying to do it all. I gave up all sources of extra income, other than a very small handful of clients. And I let go of all the "what ifs." If we were going to lose the ranch, then so be it. If we had to file bankruptcy, so be it. I had to stop *worrying* about what would happen and start taking care of myself again. I had to believe that even if those things happened, God would still take care of us.

He did.

My husband went back to carpentry. The moment he let it be known to the community that he was back in business, he had a couple of jobs lined up. We moved off the ranch, but we *still owned it*. We still had our horses. We lived only twelve minutes away.

I saw it as a new beginning. I believed we would return to the ranch again someday, once we'd gotten back on our financial feet again. Unfortunately, he saw it as an ending. He knew in his heart we'd never live there again. He didn't tell me he felt this way until much later, but he was right.

WORKBOOK

Chapter Seven Questions

Question: What are some areas where you feel resentful toward your family, coworkers, or even God because of a dream you once had, that you've not achieved?

_____
_____
_____
_____
_____
_____
_____
_____
_____
_____

Question: What characteristics does the Proverbs 31 woman have that you want to embody?

_____
_____
_____
_____
_____
_____
_____
_____
_____
_____

Question: What can you do when someone else's dream is impacting your ability to realize your own?

_____
_____
_____
_____
_____
_____

Action: Write about a sidetracked dream you have that is still important to you. What do you intend to do about it?

Chapter Seven Notes

CHAPTER EIGHT

Turning Dreams into Reality

What do you want?
When you know what you want, then you need to think about how you want to get there. You have to turn your dreams into achievable goals. You do that by:

1. *Asking God for direction.* It's important to have dreams, to know what you want to achieve in life. But if you want to live a *divinely* intentional life, you also must know what God wants for you. It's possible the two are not aligned right now.
That means surrendering your will for God's, which can be very difficult to do. After all, what good will it do for you to pursue your dreams if God has other plans? That's an act of futility! Dream away, but at the end of the day God knows what's best for you. So, include Him from the beginning. You'll be grateful for His guidance and it will save you a lot of wasted energy, believe me. I've pursued a lot of dreams that never amounted to anything, partly because I wasn't asking God what He wanted for me. I was just trying to make things happen.
When you ask God for direction, you have to *want* His guidance. You must believe that *He* knows what's best for

your life, not you—easy in theory but hard to implement! Most people I know, including myself, are stubborn. We value independence and having the freedom to make our own choices. God gives us the ability to do that. He doesn't micromanage us from His heavenly throne. We aren't mannequins dancing to His divine tune.

When our choices lead us away from our intended path, however, we can be quick to excuse it away with statements like, "I guess that just wasn't God's will for me." I've heard countless women (and men) justify failed jobs, marriages, and other decisions in this way. How convenient.

In reality, God gives us a lot of latitude to do the right or wrong thing. He also allows us to experience things that require us to develop important attributes: perseverance, resilience, determination, courage and patience. Even though we ask Him for direction and then follow where we believe He's guiding us, we will still encounter challenges and obstacles. It won't be easy. That doesn't mean it wasn't God's will. It means that life is tough for a purpose.

2. Writing your dreams down. Dreams are just dreams. They don't take you anywhere. They just stay in your head, a kaleidoscope of colorful images and ideas that may or may not be well-defined. If you want them to *happen*, you must do something with them.

Countless people have lamented to me over the years about the way their life has *turned out*, as though they had no control over it. They talk about the dreams they once had, only to acknowledge—ten, fifteen, twenty years later—that those dreams were never realized. Don't let that be you *any longer*. The only way to achieve a dream is to start the process. Pick something you want to do and write it down. Just the act of doing this uses both hemispheres of the brain.[5]

A brain that is fully engaged is now firing on all cylinders, so to speak. Far more energy is now directed towards accomplishing the dream. Using your whole brain also taps into new sources of creativity, ideas and opportunities. Writing your dream out also gives you a visual reminder that you can put anywhere, reinforcing the dream and ensuring that it becomes stored in your long-term memory.

In this stage you are simply doing a brain dump. Every idea you've ever carried around in your head goes on paper. It doesn't matter how viable you think those ideas are right now. Put them down anyway. The time for sifting and sorting comes later. If your dreams are still hazy, then work backwards. Where do you see yourself in five years? Ten years? Twenty years? What type of lifestyle do you desire? What type of career? What income do you hope for? What hobbies and/or skills would you like to spend time (and money) on? How do you see yourself contributing within your family, your church, your community? In what ways have you improved your mind, your education, your health, or your relationships? Imagining the future is a great way to start engaging your brain in the self-directed dreaming process.

3. Defining your dream. Not all dreams are viable or fit with your values and life's purpose. They might be pleasurable but not actually move you in an intentional way. You have to put your dreams into categories. Some will be essential to you, and you will want to start on them immediately. Others will be important but they can wait, or they need to wait until something else is accomplished first. Some dreams you once had will no longer seem important. Perhaps your values or circumstances have changed. Finally, you may realize that some dreams were actually things you felt you *had* to accomplish, for whatever reason. They were obligations more than dreams.

Sorting your dreams into these categories helps you to channel your energy. It also helps you to start thinking about *how* to begin accomplishing the dreams that are important to you. Ask yourself:

- What steps do I need to take to get me to this goal?
- Why is it important that I accomplish it?
- Who will benefit from me achieving it?
- How will I accomplish it?
- When will I know it's accomplished?

The answers to these questions allow you to move on to the next step.

4. Turning your dreams into intention statements and your intention statements into goals. Intention statements are a way to take a dream and begin to define it. As you write out your intentions you begin to see the necessary steps that have to happen. You also begin to get more specific about what you really *intend*.

For example, I had the dream of a certain lifestyle with my husband that I thought included living on the ranch. Writing that out as an intention statement might look like this:

> *I intend to explore different ways to make a living with our land and our arena so that we can continue to keep the ranch.*

Your intentions turn into goals once they have become well-defined: they become specific, measurable, attainable, realistic, and time-oriented (SMART), as I covered previously in chapter six.

How many times has indecision, uncertainty or fear led you to make the same mistake over and over again? SMART goals take you on a direct route from point A to point B so that you don't waste time. And the more defined your intentions the more you focus on them instead of being derailed by all the *"what if's."*

SMART goals are the big milestones you achieve as you move towards the life you want, and that God wants for you. They give you a starting point, keep you on course, and tell you when you've achieved your dreams. SMART goals also help you prioritize so that you can focus on what's most important.

Sometimes you bite off more than you can chew. You set your sights too high or make your goal too complex, only to get quickly discouraged. To avoid this, turn your SMART goal into several smaller steps or goals that you can concentrate on one at a time and give you small successes along the way.

When you turn each SMART goal into small, achievable steps, those steps help you accomplish seemingly insurmountable obstacles. Each small step moves you ever so closer to attaining your bigger goal. Before you know it, you're a fourth of the way there. Then, halfway. Then, finished.

I loved to hike in the hills behind our ranch. To get there I had to navigate through the barbed wire fencing at the back of our land and make a steep but short climb up through the sage brush to the "top." Of course, once I reached my initial ascent, I discovered there were higher points beyond. That was okay, I just enjoyed the climb. I loved the view from up there, and I loved the different rock formations that had resulted over time. I had a favorite spot I liked to hike to, where I would take a journal and pen and just sit, reflect and write.

Though I didn't know it at the time, the summer of 2013 was to be my last actually living on the ranch. I spent many afternoons up in those hills that summer, thinking about life—about what I wanted and what I didn't want.

As I reflected and wrote about those things, I began to dream again. I began to remember the professional dream I'd once had, of writing and creating courses and programs.

My dream started to take shape again on the pages of my journal. I also started thinking again about the life I'd imagined for my husband and me before we'd bought the ranch. It wasn't that I didn't enjoy the ranch or want it. I just didn't see us keeping it under our current circumstances. So I began to think of ways to change that.

- I took my ideas that I'd generated during my hikes and put them on 3x5 cards.
- I categorized them.
- I wrote out professional goals, lifestyle goals, financial goals and more.
- I put those cards by my bed so that I could review them every night before I went to sleep, and again each morning.
- I created a vision board—a collection of pictures and phrases—that I could look at daily, reminding me of what I was trying to achieve.
- I began to think about how to implement each goal, and I discussed them with my husband.

Some ideas never made it off the table. Others we tried. One idea we pursued was to turn part of our land into a trailer park for horse owners. Part of our land dipped down and out of sight from our arena. That seemed like a perfect place to put in a separate entryway off the highway. We could become landlords yet still live on the ranch. Perhaps renters might even want to take riding lessons and rent arena space. The possibilities seemed endless and I felt the stirrings of hope again.

I put together a business plan to take to the bank. We contacted the Department of Transportation and received approval for a second entryway. We hired engineers to survey the area for well placement and septic, and we hired a backhoe to dig for percolation tests. Then we ran into problems. The trailer park idea might have worked if it weren't for the fact that the percolation tests failed; the location wouldn't support a large enough septic system. In addition, the cost of another well would be prohibitive. Finally, the bank denied us the loan because they felt it might be challenging to find enough renters who were looking for horse property.

Back to square one.

The big problem, however, was that we were trying to figure out how to keep the ranch without really clarifying what we both wanted. And as it turned out, we both wanted to keep the ranch, but for different reasons. I wanted to keep the ranch because it made my husband happy to live there. He wanted to keep it because it was part of how he viewed himself and the life he wanted to lead. I still believed that his happiness would be my happiness too.

The ranch, however, wasn't something I felt particularly passionate about. I enjoyed aspects of living out there, but I didn't *have* to live there. My identity wasn't tied to it. I was more concerned about financial solvency—being able to afford the place and still enjoy life.

The other problem and probably the biggest, was that I was defining the goal *alone*. For many reasons, I felt that it was up to me to generate ideas and figure out the "how to" aspects of keeping the ranch. While I would discuss those with my husband, we never actually talked about what we both really wanted or why. We were pursuing the same goal, but for different purposes. I had made my husband's happiness my responsibility. The goals I was pursuing were in pursuit of his dream, at the expense of mine.

5. *Focusing on what you can do, not what you can't.* Not every dream you have is realistic. Part of that may be because your dream is dependent on things that are out of your control. Ask yourself, *"Can I achieve this on my own or do I need someone else's support, approval, money, etc.?"*

If the answer is yes, then go for it.

If the answer is no—if you can't do it on your own—that doesn't necessarily mean you shouldn't pursue it. It does mean, however, that you need to be realistic about what you can accomplish. Without another's support you will be limited. Finding effective ways to communicate what you want to accomplish is essential in obtaining support. However, you may encounter resistance, especially at first. When that happens, keep your focus on what *you* can do, so that you will be less likely to feel discouragement, frustration and even resentment. Your own performance needs to be the measurement of your success as opposed to outcomes that are beyond your control.

Outcomes beyond your control are outcomes that rely on what others do. Will they support you or not? Will they complete their task(s) on time or not? Will they show up when needed or not?

That summer of 2013 I was trying to control *everything*. I felt that I had to, but I resented it as well. I was also trying to hold onto something that wasn't realistic given our current circumstances.

The idea of owning rentals, however, was still

appealing to me. I talked my husband into investing in a real estate program, which ultimately led to us purchasing back our previous home at a much lower price than we'd sold it six years earlier. It wasn't hard for me to see what a good investment that was. The terms of the purchase, however, required that we live in the house.

I was fine with that; more than fine actually. If we could find a renter for the ranch, it meant lowering our personal mortgage and being closer to town. That made practical sense to me and gave me hope that we might be able to pull out of the financial hole we'd dropped into.

For my husband, however, it meant the end of his dream. Even though he was at the ranch virtually every day taking care of horses, irrigating hay and tending to things, it wasn't the same for him.

While I was regaining hope and purpose, he was hurting, though I didn't know it at the time.

It was working. We were making income. We didn't need to use our savings as much. My husband had his construction work, his horses, and the ranch to manage. I had a "new" house with repairs and renovations I could work on, inside and out, and a small handful of clients. My back pain was lessening.

Life seemed to be settling into a better routine for us, and we were experiencing some small "wins." My hope for the future was being restored.

6. *Visualizing success.* How often do you *imagine* what life will be like once your goal is accomplished? What will change? How will life improve? How will you be different? What will you think, feel and do differently once this goal has been accomplished?

The more you visualize your goal being accomplished and associate strong positive emotions with it, the greater your likelihood of success.[6] That's because it's a form of mental rehearsal. Every time you go over the process of accomplishing your goal, you are reviewing, refining and practicing success.

The distance between you and your dream might seem impossibly huge. But once you start setting goals you are actively closing that distance. You are drawing your dream toward you. Doing this changes your perspective. When something seems far away it's hard to connect it to your daily life. But when you visualize what it will be like, you allow yourself to experience the dream as your *current* reality.

Visualization comes very naturally to me. I spend a lot of time thinking about my life now and the life I want. I always have. When the time came to move off the ranch, I was already visualizing my way back! I could see exactly how that would happen—how we would become solvent again through our real estate investments and other ventures—and that when we did move back, we would finally be able to build the log home we'd dreamt of building. I even designed it in my mind with a basement apartment for another tenant. We'd already moved in a renter to our loft apartment in the arena and we'd started discussing the possibility of converting our office space below into another apartment. It all seemed very doable to me.

I was to find out later, however, that the day we drove away from the ranch to our new home my husband sensed, somehow, that we would never return to live there. That was to have a profoundly negative impact on us. I was looking forward. He was looking back. Neither of us was talking about it.

When we acquired another piece of real estate in 2014, a triplex, I *visualized* us moving even closer to the dream of keeping the ranch. Unfortunately, my husband saw the headache of more renters, vacancy challenges, and eventual repairs to an older building that would have to be done. I focused on us having a viable retirement plan whereas before there'd been none. He focused on having to go back to construction, which he'd intentionally walked away from years before. I didn't mind the challenges of being a landlord because I knew we needed to learn. He saw only the problems. He missed living on the ranch.

Turning your dreams into goals can be challenging enough. When you and your partner have different visions, it becomes virtually impossible. It was to be a few years, however, before I realized that we weren't working together to achieve the same things. He was saying the right things and going through the motions, but in reality, he was only trying to keep me happy. Internally he was grieving for what he felt he'd lost.

7. Finding support. You can't do life alone. God didn't intend that at all. We all need the support of others. Some people are already predisposed to be sympathetic and supportive of what you are trying to do. Others are not.

The support and encouragement of people who believe in what you are trying to do is essential to accomplishing your dreams. You may also need their time and energy, their expertise and even their financial backing.

Don't be afraid to ask for that support. If, however, you don't feel supported in your dreams *by the people who matter to* you, you need to find out why.

The fastest way to getting the support you want and need is to *believe you already have it.* That is, you must assume positive intent from those who love you. They *want* to support you, they *want* you to realize your dreams and they *want* you to be happy. They just need to understand how they can do that.

Unfortunately, a lot of the time we assume that when someone tells us "no" that they don't care, or that they're intentionally trying to undermine or hurt us. That negative mindset affects the way we communicate with them and others. We may become guarded and defensive. We might blame and accuse them of not caring about us.

Assuming negative intent the next time you ask for support affects the *way* you ask. It changes your tone, your facial expression, your posture and most certainly the words you use.

On the other hand, assuming positive intent requires you to analyze why you may not have received support in the past. If this person genuinely cares about your wellbeing and success, then what other reasons might there be for him/her saying no? Were you clear enough about what you needed? Did you explain how their support is essential to you and how your success would positively impact you and others? Did you show gratitude for their previous support?

> Never ascribe to malice that which can be adequately explained by ignorance.
> **—Unknown**

Don't assume you know people's motives. Unless you have overwhelming *proof* to the contrary, choose to believe that people will support you when they truly understand how they can.

If you don't have support, find it. Make new relationships, change jobs, change your environment if necessary.

When the oil and gas industry bottomed out in Wyoming in 2015, my husband could no longer find enough work to sustain us. Two things happened as a result: he had to go to Texas to work for his brother for a month while I had to stay and maintain the properties and see my few clients. It was during the time he was gone that I posed the idea to him of moving back to Texas.

This was not something I'd ever thought I would want. I couldn't wait to leave Texas eighteen years earlier, but circumstances had changed. We were traveling extremely long distances every other weekend to go to church, as our nearest congregation was in Utah, over five hours away. We'd started doing this six years earlier, after a split in our church left us without a congregation in all of Wyoming!

It had already taken a huge toll on us, physically and financially. Now, with him gone, I really felt the effects of being so alone week after week, especially since it was winter, which made it much harder to travel.

It's not that I didn't have friends of course. Some of my closest friends lived within miles of me. But not having a church family nearby was very difficult.

I began to question why we were still so committed to living in Wyoming. Things were challenging between my husband and I even though neither of us was trying to define why. I began to ask myself, *"Wouldn't it make more sense to move closer to family?"* We both had relatives living in Texas, and we could have a similar life with a better economy and a large congregation to attend.

We had many discussions about it, about the pros and cons of moving. In the end, the decision to move was mutual, or so I thought.

Looking back, I can see now that I was longing for the support of family and church that was missing, even though it would mean leaving the close friends I had in the area. As it turned out, that became crucial as other life events unfolded.

8. *Developing healthy habits.* Perhaps one reason why you don't feel supported is because your loved ones doubt your intentions. If you talk a lot about what you intend, but you find it challenging to follow through, it may be that they've stopped listening to your ideas.

Unfortunately, too many of us love to dream, but not much else. We wake up years later, mentally and emotionally, only to find that our lives haven't turned out at *all* the way we imagined. Reaching a goal requires more than just imagination. It takes *effort*!

Habits will make or break you. It doesn't matter what you *intend*, it matters what you do. Your goals are only as good as the habits you have in place that will either support or sabotage your intentions.

So:

- Don't say you're going to quit your job and start your own business, but instead come home every day and complain about your boss.
- Don't say you're going to lose twenty pounds as you reach for the potato chips.
- Don't say you intend to work out more, then watch Netflix instead.
- Don't say you're going to get out and socialize more with friends but then hang out on social media all night.

You are what you do.

Bad habits are dream killers every time.

Not all dreams come true, nor should they. Dreams needed to be sifted and sorted through like everything else. Some float to the top because of their importance, some fall to the bottom because they aren't viable.

A Dream Worth Pursuing

We didn't keep the ranch as it turns out, but the pursuit of that dream still had merit. It taught me some important things about myself. It helped me to evaluate what mattered most and what I was willing to do, or not do, to achieve it.

When you have a dream worth pursuing, then go for it. Don't give up when the journey gets tough. Persevere. If necessary, redefine what you're wanting and then start again. Be realistic. Aim for the stars but be awed and amazed if you *"only"* get to the moon. The view from there is pretty spectacular too, or so I'm told.

WORKBOOK

Chapter Eight Questions

Question: Are you focusing on what you can do to accomplish your dreams, or on things you can't control?

_____
_____
_____
_____
_____
_____
_____
_____
_____
_____

Question: Who in your life is supportive of you accomplishing your dreams? Who is not?

_____
_____
_____
_____
_____
_____
_____
_____
_____
_____
_____

Action: Take one dream and turn it into several intention statements. Then, turn each intention into a SMART goal.

Chapter Eight Notes

CHAPTER NINE

Oops! You've Lost Your Way

By 2016 my life seemed to be *back on track*. That is, I had some clearly defined goals and I was working toward achieving them.

One of those goals was to relocate to Texas. By this time the ranch had been on the market for almost a year. While the triplex sold quickly, we still had our house to sell as well.

I found myself slowing drifting off my intentional path, an inevitability that happens to everyone.

But why?

Identifying Obstacles to Intentional Living

One of the greatest obstacles to intentional living is *yourself*.

It's a fact of life that we all get derailed from the intentional living track at times. When we do, we have to make course corrections. What caused us to derail in the first place?

Questions will do that. Questions that, when asked in a certain way, hinder your ability to focus on God's wonderful design for your life and live with full intention. They create doubt and uncertainty about things you can't change or control.

That's because, sometimes, your brain travels back to the past. It goes back to your first awareness that someone didn't actually like you as a person. It goes back to your first encounter with a bully, your memories of parents fighting, or that boy that said he liked you too but never called. It remembers all the times you didn't fit in, were made fun of, put down. It recalls every relationship with a man that went sour, every poor decision you've ever made, every setback or failure. Then your brain begins to ask "Why?"

> *Why did that happen?*
> *Why did he do that?*
> *Why did I do that?*
> *Why did God allow that?*

Sometimes you ask because you have unresolved emotions about the past. Sometimes the past creates uncertainty about the future. Past mistakes might generate doubt in yourself or others.

Sometimes you just have a curiosity about how things might have turned out differently.

Sometimes you ask because you can't let go.

The problem is, when you ask "why" about something that's already occurred, you exert a lot of mental and emotional energy on something that's over. It is what it is. That sounds trite. No matter how many times you revisit the past, there's no changing it.

You can also ask "why" about situations in the present, as I was doing that summer. I didn't understand *why* there weren't clear indications that the decision to move was the right one. If it was the right choice, w*hy* weren't things flowing smoother? It made me second guess God and once again I found myself feeling anxious.

However, asking "why?" does serve a purpose when it comes to understanding your current motives. In that context it challenges you to think about what your intentions are and how they're connected to the future. For example:

> *Why am I doing this?*
>
> *Why is this important to me?*
>
> *Why will this matter later?*

Asking *why* in this context adds meaning and purpose to what you're doing. If I'd asked "why" in these ways, I could have kept my focus on the original reasons for deciding to move. They were still valid, even though not everything was happening as quickly or seamlessly as I wanted.

Instead of letting God be in charge, I was trying to take over, and doing a lousy job.

Sometimes, instead of dwelling on the past, we worry about the future. I am an idealist. I imagine my *ideal* all the time—my ideal home, career, marriage, friendships, relationship with God, etc. There are so many ways for me to mentally jump ahead to the life I want. That's not necessarily a bad thing. It helps me to get clarity about what I want and need to be doing *now*. Sometimes, though, it also keeps me from living intentionally. That happens when I begin asking "what if…"

> *What if this doesn't work out?*
>
> *What if I fail?*
>
> *What if I succeed?*

What if I don't have enough money?

What if they won't like me?

What if something terrible happens?

Asking "what if" in these ways only leads you to imagine the worst. How many times have you found yourself overreacting to something that hasn't happened, or had make-believe conversations with people about situations you've only imagined?

I'm guilty of that. I have to catch myself all the time. Then I stop and think, "What are you doing? You're reacting to something that is likely never going to happen!"

"What if" questions, in this way, only take you down a path of fear.

It's important to note that the things we worry about rarely, if ever, turn out the way we think. Nothing has ever happened the way I worry it will, in the exact way I imagined. I still tend to catastrophize it. Then I have an emotional reaction to that potential catastrophe, which can lead me to act in impulsive or reactive ways. Almost always it robs me of the ability to stay focused on what I can do, right now, instead of worrying about things out of my control.

Of course, "what if?" doesn't have to be bad. After all, *what if* you used it to imagine wonderful outcomes, to dream of all the future possibilities that God has in store for you?

What if you used it to create energy and momentum in your life instead of doubt and inertia?

What if you actually began focusing on today instead of getting stuck in tomorrow?

That summer when we finally moved to Texas, not everything worked out the way we hoped. Two of our three properties had not sold yet. We decided to find renters and at the last moment found a family to rent our home, but the two apartments at the ranch were empty.

Still, we were committed to going. We'd sold everything we could that wasn't feasible to bring with us, including our horses, a painful decision for my husband that only reinforced the loss he was already feeling. The rest of our belongings we would either use to furnish our small, one-bedroom apartment or store with family.

Another question we tend to ask is "when."

I found myself struggling with questions like:

> *When will our properties sell?*
>
> *When will we find renters for the ranch?*
>
> *When will be able to buy another home?*

Asking "when" in this way means you're just—*waiting*. You're waiting for circumstances to change, others to change, life to change. Waiting is passive, not proactive. When you're waiting you're not "doing." Then, someday, you wake up and wonder why your life hasn't turned out the way you wanted it to.

Instead, ask "when" about things you can do *right now*. Using "when" as a time marker for your goals looks like this:

> *When do I need to accomplish this by?*
>
> *When will I know it is accomplished?*
>
> *When will I know that conditions are right for me to _____?*

The move was easier for me in some ways. Though many people find change scary, I'm always thinking, "What's next?" I love change. Professionally or personally, I can't wait until the next project or event.

Sometimes, though, I pin my happiness on future achievement instead of enjoying the process. My brain wants to rush ahead and anticipate how much better it will be *when* _____. It wants to worry about what it will be like in the future if things don't go the way I think they should. I begin to feel impatient.

Of course, things never happen fast enough.

Jesus addressed this very thing with His disciples. "Therefore do not worry about tomorrow, for tomorrow will worry about its own things. Sufficient for the day *is* its own trouble" (Matthew 6:34). That's easy to read and say, but really hard to implement. I've derailed myself many times over the years, worrying about things that have yet to occur.

What about you?

There really aren't any "bad" questions. You just need to ask them in the right way, about the right things. Questions are actually very useful, when they lead to clear answers. They can generate epiphanies and breakthroughs in many aspects of life. They can bring you clarity. The key though is to ask those questions about the *right* things. The right things are things you have 100% control over. When you focus on them, then every question becomes meaningful.

Asking questions about things you can't change or control only encourages three things: doubt, fear, and worry. They will derail you every time.

A Closer Look at Anxiety

Anxiety, doubt, and worry often generate negativity, and when you are negative, you are exerting a lot of energy on things that have either already happened, haven't happened, and may never happen. According to an article written by Neringa Antanaityte, Consultant and Trainer at TLEX Institute Europe, a study by the National Science

Foundation found that the average person has about 12,000 to 60,000 thoughts per day, and that 80% of those thoughts are negative, and 95% are the same repetitive thoughts as the day before.[7]

That's a lot of negativity, which can lead to mental and emotional paralysis. When that happens, you feel unable to think clearly, unable to take any confident action that might help you break free. What a tremendous psychological burden and a waste of energy!

How can you feel positive about your life when you are consumed by negativity?

You can't!

Most of the things you are anxious about are *not real*. They are about outcomes you *imagine* will happen in the future that you don't want, even though your sense of fear is very real, and can be very debilitating.

There are three components to anxiety: your worrying thoughts, your emotions, and your physiological response. *Your body responds to fear, real or imagined!* When you are fearful about imagined outcomes, you are putting yourself through unnecessary suffering.

Shifting Focus

What if you took that energy and focused it on what really matters—the here and now? What could you be doing or accomplishing instead? Think about it. Isn't a dream simply an imagined future outcome that you *do* want? The only difference between a fear and a dream is that one represents what you don't want, while the other represents what you do.

What do you *want* to accomplish? Focus on what you *do* want instead of what you *don't*. Then, focus on what you can do to get yourself there.

When you concentrate on the tangible steps that you have control over, that helps to shift you back to your goals, which pushes past the fear. Once you do, you've begun to focus on your dreams again. You've begun to place your mental energy on how to move yourself forward. You feel more purposeful. You've put yourself in a position to *observe* your fears and then *use* those observations to focus on your dreams and goals instead.

What a difference it makes when you begin to channel your energy into areas of your life that you can actually change. The problem is, this is *hard to do*. Very few of us are able to live in the moment, without doubt, worry, or stress ever derailing us. That's because things happen that cause us to get off course.

Let's call those *triggers*.

The Never-ending Cycle

A trigger is anything in life that sets in motion a cycle of thoughts, feelings and reactions. Most triggers are not in our control and occur naturally throughout each day.

Something happens and we immediately interpret it in a certain way. That interpretation, which generates a thought process, leads to an emotional response. These thoughts and emotions occur almost simultaneously. Together they generate a behavioral response. If we interpret the event in a negative or fearful way we may cry, yell or say something we don't mean.

Many times, we blame our feelings on others. We say things like "I can't help the way I feel." "They just make me feel so angry," or "I wouldn't feel that way if he/she would just...." We may feel powerless to change our feelings. But we are not powerless at all. In fact, there are three things that we are always responsible for: our thoughts, feelings, and actions/reactions. When we blame circumstances or others for the way we think, feel, or behave, we are abdicating our responsibility to change. Instead we become a victim of those circumstances.

When I realized that I was spiraling back to a place of fear I had to first identify why. I realized that I was dwelling on things I could do nothing about. Those worrying thoughts about the future created frustration and fear. There was a lot I couldn't control, a lot of uncertainty about things—money, renters, the move itself, and what life would look like in the big city. Dwelling on those uncertainties led me to feel helpless and anxious.

Triggers can set us on a cycle of reactionary living if we don't slow down and become aware of them. When we realize what our triggers are, we can use that knowledge to try to work through them or avoid them. It's also important to recognize that it's our *interpretation* of a situation that generates our thoughts, and so on.

If we can view a situation differently, we can generate more proactive thoughts—thoughts that lead to problem-solving behaviors and solutions instead of reactionary responses that only trigger further negativity. When we first attempt to do this, to become aware of our triggers and our interpretation of them, it's usually after the fact. We've already reacted. It's too late to go back and undo what we've already said or done, but it's still important to know.

Questions like "What was I thinking?" "How could I have thought about that differently?" and "How might I have felt and reacted instead?" are useful. Each time you do this you are creating greater self-awareness. After all, you can't change what you aren't aware of!

Think of it this way. All that negative self-talk is like a CD playing on repeat in your head—but on mute. You are still reacting to all that negativity, but you aren't always consciously aware you're doing it.

Once you learn what triggers you have and how you typically respond to those triggers, you can begin to change the cycle. You do this with *thought changing* and *thought stopping* techniques. For example, if you've come to recognize that you have a tendency to think the worst about situations and you catch yourself mid-cycle, you need to tell yourself to "STOP!" The hurt and damage you are causing yourself by spiraling down that path are immeasurable.

Secondly, you must actively work to change that negative thought cycle with more productive thinking. I'm not suggesting you *lie* to yourself or pretend that things aren't difficult or stressful. But tweaking our thoughts, even slightly, can have a tremendous impact, especially over time.

When I decided to shift my focus to the move itself, my thoughts, feelings, and actions changed. I told myself to stop worrying about what I couldn't change. It would work out, it always had, and it would this time as well. I didn't need to know how, I just needed to trust that God would take care of us. Those thoughts calmed me down and allowed me to work proactively on packing up our home, on determining what could fit in our small apartment and what needed to be stored. We had decided that, since this would be a transitional year, we would take the opportunity to spend the next ten months in a theological program that our church taught yearly. We had enough savings, if we were careful, to take the year off from work.

Preparing to be a student again was exciting for me. It gave me something positive and proactive to do and took my attention off of the things that I couldn't change. My worries were still there, but I was choosing to not focus on them as much.

Self-Focused Behaviors

There are other aspects of the *self* that can derail us. Self-focused behaviors can also serve as obstacles and can manifest in a variety of harmful ways. They are self-interest, self-protection, self-destruction, and self-justification. Let's take a closer look at each one of these.

Self-interest

Intentional living is also balanced living. A woman who is balanced is a woman who is aware of her needs and is taking care of them in a healthy way, without neglecting her loved ones. Unfortunately there's those of us who go around thinking, *"It's all about me!"* We can be quick to label others as narcissistic. Certainly we all know someone who fits the criteria, but we all have the tendency to be selfish at times. When we focus primarily on our own needs, sometimes to the detriment or exclusion of others, we quickly become unbalanced. When this happens, it can be an indication that your spiritual and emotional tanks have been running on empty for a long time.

Melissa married Gary at 22, even though she was in love with another man that her family didn't approve of. She knew on some level that she was on the rebound and almost called off the wedding. Gary had a very different personality. They had very little in common, and they fought all the time. It became a pattern—fight, make up, fight, make up. They fought so much that they decided to not bring children into the situation.
Looking back, she sees now that she was just going through the motions, trying to do what she thought everyone else wanted for her. It was so intimidating to think about what people might think, how disappointed they would be, if she left him. At times the confusion and anguish of her situation was so paralyzing that she would just curl up in a fetal position and cry.
It can be easy to go into blame mode when things get this bad. You may be waiting for someone else to meet

your needs. You may feel angry, resentful, and even bitter. Your thoughts likely follow a predictable pattern.

> *"No one's meeting my needs anymore."*
>
> *"I feel lonely and unloved."*
>
> *"This is so unfair."*

This kind of self-interest is detrimental to living intentionally because it is focused primarily on how things affect *your* well-being, instead of considering yourself within a larger context. It focuses on what others are (or aren't) doing to make you happy, instead of what you can do for yourself.

When you look beyond yourself and start thinking about what life is like for those around you, it changes your perspective. It makes you a more thoughtful, caring, and considerate person, one who is more likely to be *intentionally* kind, gentle, and loving to others and yourself.

Self-protection

On one hand, self-protection is a good thing. You don't want to be a physical or emotional doormat, letting people push or pull you around to suit their purposes. That's not what I'm talking about, however.

The type of self-protection I'm referring to is what happens when you've learned from experience that people *can* hurt you. When the world becomes a scary, uninviting, overwhelming place, you may want to pull away, or build a "wall" that keeps people at an emotional distance. In other words, you live in fear of being hurt, rejected, and betrayed. Eventually you come to anticipate the worst: from people, from life, from yourself.

It's natural to want to protect yourself from anybody ever hurting you again. Unfortunately, when you push people away because you're afraid, you also prevent good things from happening too. You don't get to pick and choose. A wall is a wall and it can get lonely behind it.

Gillian struggled to feel heard and understood after her divorce. Her marriage to Cliff was a difficult one, made worse by the choices she made trying to cope with his erratic, often abusive treatment.

Long work hours, constant travel and never-ending stress on the home front were made "easier" with alcohol. Until, of course, her drinking became its own problem. In danger of losing her job and her children, she felt ridden with guilt and shame, even though she knew that the divorce wasn't all her fault.

Her work transferred her to a new location, but the damage to her credibility had been done, even though her work performance was exemplary.

It didn't help that her ex-husband never missed an opportunity to slander her to others, who were quick to believe his twisted version of events. Former friends aligned themselves with him. Some accused her, without cause, of unethical behavior at work. Her employer was even dragged into the post-divorce mess in a well-meaning attempt to mediate, that only made things worse. Even her children began distancing themselves.

Yet most of time when she tried to explain what her marriage had been like she would feel shut down. "They didn't want to hear about that," she shared. "They only wanted me to acknowledge my mistakes and what I was doing to change. That was really hard. I knew I'd screwed up. But I felt a complete unwillingness from people to hear me, or to empathize with what I'd gone through."

Gillian felt alone. She attempted to get help for her drinking but struggled to give it up. Depression set in and she began isolating herself. She didn't know who she could trust, so she trusted no one. She buried herself in her work then would crash on the weekends, sometimes sleeping all day in her dark apartment.

She felt like a leper at work. She went to church weekly but felt people's stares and was certain they were judging her. It was difficult to know who she could open up to, so she stopped trying. Some would tell her she needed to be more social. She knew they were right, but her thoughts were a never-ending cycle that kept her trapped in fear.

There are two possible responses to fear: movement or paralysis. You can face your fears and move forward anyway, or you can freeze. But when you freeze, too terrified to take risks—personal, professional, financial—you remain stuck. How many times, and in how many situations, have you, like Gillian, come to expect the worst? When your boss says he wants to meet with you privately, do you immediately assume you're in trouble? When someone hurts or disappoints you, do you tell yourself "I should have known that would happen?" Do you anticipate the worst, and by doing so, create that very thing? You may think you're protecting yourself from getting hurt again by not wanting or expecting too much. In reality, loneliness, discouragement and hopelessness are the fruits of self-protection.

Self-protection that results from not wanting to get hurt again, or not wanting to trust in others because you've been let down before, is understandable. But the past is not an indicator of how things are now or will be in the future, unless you set it up to be. Life is filled with situations that are going to feel like emotional setbacks—and sometimes they actually are. This is where resiliency is such an important quality—the ability to recover from challenges as quickly as possible. Think of a rubber band. Life's going to stretch you out at times. But your ability to stay *elastic* is essential to realizing your dreams.

Yesterday's gone, and tomorrow's not here yet. When

you catch yourself dwelling on the past or imagining the worst and you're wanting to shield yourself from further hurt, *gently* bring yourself back to the present and on what you can think, feel, and do, today, that will alleviate (or lessen) your anxiety. Then, do it.

Self-destruction

One of the ways we can get in our own way is by engaging in destructive habits. Though we may be terrified of being vulnerable again, God did not intend us to live a life of solitude. Intimacy with others does involve risk. So what do some do? They fill the void that loneliness brings in some way. Perhaps they overindulge in food, alcohol, spending, or entertainment, to name a few. Maybe they keep ourselves so busy that they don't have time to think about their loneliness.

In some ways, when my husband and I started our theological classes in Texas, our routine changed. Evenings were devoted to helping him study and memorize material for weekly quizzes. He'd never been a strong student, so this was challenging for him, and I was happy to help. In other ways, we'd slipped into a pattern of behavior that was very destructive to our relationship.

Many things had happened that we could never discuss without conflict. We avoided talking about them as a result. We didn't talk at all about our relationship, only the mundane aspects of daily life. He had his hurts that he kept to himself. I had mine. We were two people who had begun drifting apart years earlier without seeing it. Then, when it became apparent we had problems, instead of working together to find resolution, he became accusatory and I withdrew.

I did that in a variety of ways. I'd always loved to read or watch movies as a way of clearing my mind at the end of a long day of listening to clients' problems. Whereas before I'd been able to achieve balance, now it became a way to escape.

My husband would complain that I never talked to him anymore. I'd come to believe that talking about anything meaningful was not going to happen, so what was the point? It felt like a waste of time. I wasn't happy, nor was he. I didn't see that efforts to resolve things were leading to any meaningful change. So I convinced myself that the status quo was good enough.

Anything that sabotages your efforts to be intentional and robs you of peace of mind is destructive. It could be a time waster, a negative environment or relationship, or a habit that's counterproductive. When you recognize what you're doing but you *choose* to continue doing it anyway, then it becomes a form of self-destruction, as I came to experience firsthand.

Self-justification

Sometimes, though, it takes a while to realize this. We lie to ourselves. We make excuses, like:

"Well at least I'm…."

"It could be worse…."

"This isn't really a problem, not like so and so."

"It's not a big deal. I could stop if I wanted to."

"It's my life. I'm not hurting anyone or anything by it."

It's so easy to convince yourself of the "rightness" of what you're doing, partly because it's so hard to stop doing it.

I was definitely justifying my behaviors, my reasons for mentally and emotionally "checking out" of my marriage. I thought that changing our environment—moving to a new state, being closer to family—might help us make those changes. In reality, the changes we needed were internal.

Change is hard. We innately don't want to change, even when we may say we do. Change means getting off that familiar path. It means becoming more intentional, and then going to work.

Enemies of Divinely Intentional Living

Two other obstacles that can quickly derail us from intentional living that I'll address briefly are *societal* and *satanic* influences.

We are all pushed and pulled at times by external forces. Knowing what those are is important, so that you can combat them as needed.

Western culture sends women false messages all the time. It tells us we deserve all we want, and that we can have it all. It tells us we should be independent, but not *too* independent; strong, but not *too* strong; capable, but not *too capable.* It puts most of its emphasis on showing us how to look beautiful but not *act* in beautiful ways.

Knowing how society has shaped your thinking as a woman is critical to being intentional. Are you just going along with what's popular and trendy to fit in and be "normal," or are you defined by a different standard—a godly standard—that doesn't shift over time?

Never forget that Satan is your spiritual enemy. He uses lies, fear, societal pressures, past wounds, and present hurts to keep you separated from God. The last thing he wants is for you to live a divinely intentional life. He will use everything at his disposal to pull you off course, and he attempts to sabotage you daily (Revelation 12:10).

As Christians we call this spiritual warfare (Ephesians 6:10–13). Life isn't a playground and we aren't on a merry-go-round. Sometimes it's very difficult, and painful. If we allow him to, Satan will use those difficult times against us.

Unhealthy Relationships

Finally, if you are struggling to stay intentional you need to consider your relationships.

Not all relationships are equal, nor are they all supportive of the intentional changes you are making. There are many factors that explain this. First you have to identify which relationships are healthy, and which may be toxic.

Healthy relationships are with people who motivate you to get off your familiar, complacent path. They challenge your thinking. They encourage you to grow, learn and achieve more. They call you out on things that you are doing to damage yourself. As painful as that may be, sometimes that's what we need—not just an accountability partner, but someone who is willing to stand by our side and fight our battles with us. We need someone who will help us recognize it's a battle against ourselves as well as a spiritual battle.

Healthy people embrace your strengths and your weaknesses. They don't sugarcoat things for you, but when they do offer feedback it's with love and compassion. If you surround yourself with people who are constantly validating you, you're doing yourself a disservice. That might make you feel good, but it does nothing to help you improve or become more intentional.

Some relationships, however, are damaging and destructive to intentional living. How can you know the difference?

Toxic people are:

- Pushy and demanding. They almost always get their way. They will use criticism, negative feedback and other emotionally manipulative ways to coerce you into doing what they want. They are not interested in your welfare, but in what they can get from you.
- Self-centered. They want to talk about things you don't want to talk about. Topics are often about them and their problems. They may listen for a brief moment before bringing the conversation back to them.
- Dangerous. They may encourage you to spend money you don't have, act impulsively and do things that go against your values. They may be controlling and even abusive.
- Unsupportive and unreliable. They want you when they have needs, but they find excuses when the reverse is true. You can't rely on them when things get tough.

A toxic relationship can leave you feeling confused and exhausted, rather than satisfied and content. If you are in a toxic relationship, it won't matter how intentional you try to be. Sooner or later the other person will undermine your efforts.

The Rest of the Story

Things shifted for Melissa when she took a class that made her think about her future. She realized that she was not realizing her full potential, but that it was up to her, not her husband, to change that.

Scared but determined, she separated and ultimately divorced. "I wasn't afraid to be alone, or about money, "she recalls. "It was what everyone was going to think about me." Once she took the leap to make changes within herself there was no turning back. "Honestly, I wish I'd had the courage to not marry him in the first place," she admits. "You think you can't afford to change your circumstances, whatever they are, but you really can't afford not to. You are responsible for you! Even if you've made decisions you don't like, it's up to you to get out of them."

Happily married now to the man she first loved; they have four beautiful children. Though her second marriage has had its ups and downs too, she says she hardly ever worries now because it's a wasted emotion. Being in an unhealthy marriage taught her not to care so much about what other people think. "You need to figure out a way to conquer your fear. There's no easy way except to just jump and do it. You've got to be willing to leap, and care about yourself and not listen to everyone else's expectations for you. Have enough respect for yourself to listen to yourself and God first."

Gillian's story has evolved as well. After a couple of false starts with other men, she reached out to a friend who was going through something similar, to offer support. Before she knew it, that friendship had blossomed into love. Common hurts brought them together, but it was their mutual values, interests, and instant chemistry that cemented their relationship.

Looking back on the past few years, Gillian reflects on the mistakes she's made. "I knew where I wanted to be but there was this major mountain in the middle that seemed insurmountable. In those moments of self-doubt, it's easy to get into relationships that aren't constructive. You aren't ready, even though you need and crave the support. But if you can build a healthy relationship—even believe that it's possible and that you're not a loser—it can really turn your life around. It takes time and effort. It's not a silver bullet or a quick fix. Eventually you start viewing yourself and others in healthier ways."

Finding love again has changed Gillian in many positive ways. She's intentionally trying to view people differently. She knows now that people don't always realize how much you're still struggling—especially when you aren't opening up—so they aren't sensitive to your pain. And though she admits it's still hard, she's reaching out to old friends and trying to make new ones. She's hopeful about her future, about the relationship she's now in, and she's making better decisions. Every day she feels stronger, as she focuses on what *can* be instead of what *was*. She's dreaming again.

Never Give Up

Obstacles occur for everyone. They're unavoidable, but they can be overcome. Nothing is insurmountable (Romans 8:28). Choosing a different path, the path of living with divine intention, is the beginning of a new journey. As you move forward, you will encounter setbacks. That's just life. It's how you handle those setbacks that determines how far you get.

Don't give up. Pause to "catch your breath" if you need to. Stop and listen to God for some much needed redirection. Seek guidance from others. Redefine where you're trying to go, who you're wanting to be. Do whatever it takes to stay the course. Never, ever give up.

WORKBOOK

Chapter Nine Questions

Question: What are some negative ways that you ask questions that keep you from being intentional? How could you ask those questions in a more productive way?

_____
_____
_____
_____
_____
_____
_____
_____
_____
_____
_____

Question: What are some typical scenarios that trigger you? What thought patterns lead you to fear, anxiety, anger or frustration? How can and will you begin to change those thought patterns? How can your faith be a help to you in doing this?

_____
_____
_____
_____
_____
_____
_____
_____
_____
_____

Question: What fears do you battle most? For each fear, answer the question: What is it that I want that eliminates this fear? What dream or goal can you focus on in place of each fear?

_____
_____
_____
_____

Question: How healthy/unhealthy are your relationships right now?

Action: Review the list of the four "self" behaviors: self-interest, self-protection, self-destruction, and self-justification. For each of these "self" behaviors, evaluate areas of your life that have become subject to these obstacles. What steps do you need to take to start overcoming those "self" behaviors?

Chapter Nine Notes

CHAPTER TEN

Intentionality in Motion

You want to be happy, and when you are, it's wonderful. That's why so many people crave happiness, and why so many of us are constantly searching for it when it goes away.
It's not wrong to want to be happy. The question is: *How do you define happiness?*
The year we spent taking theology classes was a peaceful one for me overall. The stress of running a business was mostly gone. My husband had taken the year off from construction to focus on his classes, though I still had the occasional client that I worked with over the internet. Still, most of our days consisted of lectures and homework, which was an easy environment for me.
I also enjoyed being in the city after so many years of isolation in Wyoming. We'd gone from very little social interaction with our Church family, to having endless opportunities to connect with people. While our apartment was much smaller than the home we'd just moved from, it wasn't difficult for me to adjust. The sacrifice of space was outweighed by the convenience of having friends and family nearby.
I thought things seemed more peaceful between my

husband and me. I look back on that time, however, and realize that what I thought was a peaceful time was just the absence of conflict. We weren't talking about what really mattered.

We weren't talking about how he felt about leaving Wyoming, giving up his ranch, his horses, and the lifestyle he'd enjoyed there. We weren't talking about how much he hated living in the city, in a tiny apartment. He had mixed feelings about being around family that he wasn't sharing. He would complain about it periodically, but he wasn't able to verbalize *why*.

As the year progressed and our home and ranch had still not sold, I tried to discuss with him what our options might be if we graduated and still didn't have the money to buy a home. Neither of us had any answers.

Then we met some previous graduates of our theology program who had participated in our church's international volunteer program at schools in the Middle East. That led to us discussing the possibility of volunteering overseas as well.

The Jordan project was established in the 1980s in collaboration with members of the royal Jordanian family. Initially it was established to help children with mental and physical challenges but was later expanded to include the International Baccalaureate School. Volunteers who are selected are assigned to one of two schools in Amman, based on their education and experiences. Some help in a classroom setting, others may be given administrative assistant duties. Jobs depend on each school's needs at the time.

The project is a ten-month commitment. Volunteers typically go from August through May or June of the following year. Each volunteer receives a basic stipend that pays for food and other incidentals. Housing and one-way airfare are included.

We reached out to the director of the Jordan project and

he encouraged us to apply. Five months later, just as we were getting ready to graduate, we found out—along with two other graduates—that we'd been accepted for the 2017 school year in Amman, Jordan.

That summer was a whirlwind of activity as we packed up our home once again. We had to find a temporary place for our vehicles, our dog, and all our furniture. It was also an exciting time, for me at least. I'd always wanted to experience living overseas, so this was a dream come true. I looked forward to a new adventure, as well as the opportunity to explore a new country and culture and be of service in whatever position I'd be asked to work.

Though my husband and I both knew what schools we'd be working at, neither of us knew exactly what our responsibilities would be. I was determined to do whatever job I was asked to do, as I knew it would be unlikely that I'd be working in my field.

As our day of departure approached, I grew more excited. I thought my husband felt the same. He'd certainly expressed equal interest in going. We'd traveled internationally together several times in our twenty-two years together, so this wasn't a completely unfamiliar experience.

Naively, I expected only positive outcomes from this opportunity. Some unexpected curveballs, however, were definitely coming our way.

Happiness as a Byproduct

Though I certainly experienced moments of happiness as I anticipated our year in Jordan, that's not the kind of happiness I'm talking about. There's a different kind of happiness, one that's worth pursuing, but not for its own sake. Happiness that comes from fleeting pleasures will always be temporary. Sustainable happiness is a byproduct of living a certain way.

When you live with *divine intention* you are taking personal responsibility for your life. You are seeking God's will in all that you do, asking for His values to be yours, and then living by them. The kind of happiness this leads to is a state of mind. That state of mind doesn't have to change, no matter what life throws at you.

Does that sound like something worth pursuing?

It certainly does to me!

How do you actually achieve that? What are the concrete, daily steps that lead to this state of mind?

The best way to think about intentional living, in my opinion, is on a sliding scale. On one end you have your ideal: complete intentionality in everything you do, based on God's word. The other end of the scale represents emotional impulsivity—making decisions on a whim, based on what feels good in the moment. Where you are on the scale can vary from day to day, week to week, month to month, etc. Sometimes you are being very intentional about life. Other times, not so much.

The first step to being more intentional is to be aware of where you are on that scale at any given time, so that you can determine what to do about it.

Schedule two daily appointments.

There are two ways for you to become more aware of what you are doing (or not doing).

Both are essential.

First of all, God can and will reveal it to you, over time. This will only happen, however, if you have a close relationship with Him.

How do you form any relationship? You do so by spending intimate time with that person. It doesn't happen overnight—relationships aren't typically built all at once—you have to invest time and energy. You have to show up. In any good relationship, sometimes you're talking, sometimes you're listening

If you want God to show you how and where to be

more intentional, then make time for Him every day. That means carving time out for Him. Review your typical day. How and where can you best create time? Does it mean getting up a bit earlier, even though that means a little less sleep? Does it mean putting your children to bed a little earlier? Does it mean giving up some television time?

What are you willing to sacrifice for time with God?

Your relationship with God is essential to your success, and the best way to find out whether starting your day with God (or without) sets you up for success (or failure) is to try it. What changes for you when you devote that time to your relationship? Track the thoughts, emotions and actions that stem from making God your first priority.

Secondly, you must make a daily *appointment* with yourself.

Treat your appointment seriously. Be sure that this time is free from distractions or interruptions. That may mean getting out of the house (you don't have to go far; go sit in your car, or in your backyard, or walk to the park). The time of day is up to you. It should be when you are at your optimal best, not when you are exhausted and least feel like thinking about these things.

During this quiet time, reflect on your day. Think about what you want and/or need to do and why. Write those things down, as they give you a visual reminder of what you intend to accomplish. You'll also reflect on whether those daily tasks are linked to bigger goals, or not. Are you moving closer to achieving your dreams? If not, what needs to change? Are you allocating your time wisely? Are you wasting it? You may still be busy. Busy isn't necessarily better though—it's just busy.

You'll also think beyond the day. What are the priority goals that you want/need to achieve tomorrow/this week/this month or beyond? What are the potential obstacles that will come up and try to distract or discourage you from accomplishing those goals? What will you do to keep that from happening?

Evaluate how you did on achieving yesterday's priorities. Did you accomplish what you set out to do? If not, why not? What can you do better today or tomorrow? Your priorities, which reflect your values, revolve around your roles: as a Christian woman, a wife, mother, employee, business owner, daughter, sister, friend, etc. Your goals need to address each one of these roles. Some roles, however, are more important than others, and not all goals are equal in value. Knowing what to focus on first is essential to living an intentional life, instead of just a busy one. Your eye must always be on how your actions *today* are preparing you for tomorrow, beyond the physical realm.

Finally, celebrate what's working well! How will you reward yourself for a goal that's progressing or has been met? Appropriate rewards (that don't sabotage your efforts) are essential for keeping you motivated. A special treat, meal, outing, or purchase are options. You can also *postpone* doing something you typically enjoy each day, until your goal has been met. It then becomes the reward.

Remember the pyramid perspective? The pyramid determines your goals and how you prioritize your time. When you start your day off with God and take time to plan out and reflect on your day, then your other priority relationships will benefit. The second most important relationship is with yourself, because taking care of yourself is the right thing to do for you and your loved ones. The rest of the pyramid is determined by your current roles. Let's take a look at some of those in terms of how to be more intentional within each one.

Being Single

If you aren't married, make the most of being single!

Don't let yourself be rushed into a romantic relationship out of loneliness. At the same time, don't put your life on hold.

Right now you might be thinking, "It would be so nice to be married and have a partner, someone to share life with." This stage of your life, though, is a huge opportunity for self-improvement. Living intentionally means living in the moment. It means squeezing every drop out of every day, not waiting for something better around the bend. Today is what you have. Tomorrow you may be married, or you may not. So live!

Prepare yourself financially. Go buy that house if you can afford to. Don't wait until you have a spouse. Get educated. Establish your career. Make your investments. See the world. Learn to love life as it is, not as it could be.

Being Married

Then it happens. You find that special someone and you start a life together. At first it's wonderful. Then it becomes hard work.

Several years ago when I still lived in Wyoming, I had the idea of turning a grassy area in my front lawn into an extensive flower garden. The problem was, I wasn't a gardener. I didn't let that deter me though. I drew out my plans and went to work, painstakingly digging up the grass one shovel load at a time. The vision I had carried me through the hard work. It didn't even seem that hard because I was so focused on what I wanted to create.

Once the ground was dug up and rotor tilled, I applied fertilizer, then began strategically planting. I knew I wanted primarily perennials. I also wanted a rock stepping path through the length of the garden, with a fountain and a bench seat where I could sit and journal or read on nice days. I wanted it to be colorful throughout the spring and summer, which meant that I had to know what would bloom and at which times of the year. I wanted a lot of variation in plant height.

Also, I needed to achieve all this on a very limited budget. A friend gave me several Hollyhock seeds and I planted those. I dug up wild sunflowers and replanted them. Another friend gave me cuttings from his garden. As I was able to, I would go down to the local flower shop and buy a new addition, then come home and quickly plant it. I learned how to dig a deep enough hole, and then hollow out an area around the plant to retain water. I also learned how to separate the roots out of a plant that had become bound.

I dug up large rocks that I would find around the property or when I was out hiking and bring them back to use in creating my rock pathway, or in other areas for visual appeal. When the initial planting was complete, I put wood chips down to hold in the moisture.

Then, I waited. Some plants, like the Hollyhocks, didn't begin blooming for a couple of years, but it was still exciting to see them grow into small plants. Others flowered that same summer. Over the years, the garden began to really mature and take shape. It was exciting to realize the fruits of all my effort.

Then we sold the house. Six years went by during which we lived on our ranch and devoted much time and energy into building a new life out there. Then the opportunity to buy the house back came up. Only, the garden I'd worked so hard to build had been deeply neglected. Whereas it had once been a beautiful variety of color and textures, now it was overgrown and filled with weeds.

Marriage can be like that. You set out with such great anticipation and expectations. You know exactly what you want, and for a while the love you feel for each other carries you through some of the initial challenges. Then you experience setbacks. Some of them may be financial, some may be job or family related. Some may be things about your spouse that you didn't realize or chose to overlook beforehand.

Sometimes just the routine of things causes you to feel settled, even bored. Things that were new and exciting may now seem mundane. Children may come along. The sheer exhaustion of raising them often robs you of the time and energy that a marriage needs to thrive. It can be hard to prioritize your husband's needs (and yours) when you have young children clamoring for attention!

Yet intentionality within marriage means never letting go of your vision. What you wanted in the beginning is no less valid now, though it may be tempered now by certain realities. It also means understanding God's purpose for marriage. He had His own very clear vision in mind when He designed marital roles. Does your marriage live up to what God intended? Does it live up to what *you* intended when you first said, "I do"? Do you and God even want the same things?

Much like the garden I inherited when we bought our house for the second time, your marital garden requires more than just an initial planting. It requires ongoing fertilization, moisture and sunlight. It requires much weeding! You can lament over the weeds. You can blame your spouse for them, or you can get to work and start pulling.

Being a Mom

Having children can be an incredibly rewarding experience, yet can make you want to pull all your hair out in complete frustration in equal measures!

It's ironic that one of our hardest and most significant roles comes with zero training requirements. Most parents raise their children based on how they were parented, repeating what seemed to work and (hopefully!) avoiding what didn't. Despite your best efforts, you will make mistakes.

If there were a course on how to parent that guaranteed success, I wonder how many of us would actually take it. The fact is, it's impossible to avoid all the hard knocks of being a mom, because all the book knowledge in the world doesn't fully prepare you for the reality. To really learn to parent, you have to *be* a parent.

That doesn't mean you shouldn't prepare. Whether you're in the pre-parenting stage or dealing with obstinate teens, it's never too early or too late to learn solid, time-tested parenting principles.

What does it truly mean to be an intentional mom?

To be intentional, you have to know what you want to achieve. Do you want to raise children who are strong, confident, responsible and hard-working? What do you need to teach them so that they can be? How do you need to discipline them? What opportunities do you need to expose them to?

If you don't have a parenting plan, you may default to what's convenient and easy in the moment. You may make allowances for things that you shouldn't, and make compromises where you need to stand firm. You may spoil them, or parent out of guilt because of your own shortcomings.

Consider two key principles that are worth instilling in your children, first and foremost by your own example.

1. Responsibility

Responsibility isn't common these days. Children generally seem uninterested unless something's fun, entertaining or easy. Yet part of preparing children for adulthood is teaching them that life isn't all about fun and games or getting our way; there are a lot of things we do out of responsibility—even when we don't feel like it.

Things like cooking dinner, mowing the lawn, paying bills and cleaning aren't always fun, but they need to be done.

When kids are little, they often want to help. They will follow Mommy around, wiping up messes, dragging a toy vacuum around the floor and generally getting in the way. As they get older, however, the desire to help diminishes *unless* parents have cultivated it. Small, basic jobs help children learn the importance of responsibility and should be assigned beginning when children are small and continued consistently throughout their childhood.

Here are some ideas for teaching responsibility to your children:

Have realistic expectations. Set the bar high, but not so high that it exceeds your child's abilities.

Use tasks to teach life lessons. For instance, responsibilities can help teach the values of contributing to the greater good, respecting others, service and how the real world works.

Set up a routine. Kids need predictability. Giving children daily, weekly and/or monthly chores teaches them the importance of the routine nature of responsibility.

Make responsibilities personal and varied. Kids need to connect with the value behind the chore—to understand the benefits for them as well as for others. Rotating out different tasks creates competence in several areas.

2. Accountability

Being personally responsible for one's actions is hard, even for adults. Without accountability we blame others, justify our poor choices, and refuse to do things that seem *unfair* or *boring*. Intentional moms work to create a culture of accountability within the home, starting with themselves. This teaches children that every choice has consequences and that there are rules and expectations that apply to everyone.

Here are some ideas to help you teach accountability:

Positive and negative consequences. Use positive consequences (rewards) to encourage right behavior, and negative consequences (discipline) to discourage wrong behavior. Rewards should be used carefully and temporarily because they shouldn't be the main motivation for learning to be responsible.

Consequences should be consistent and effective. Find out what motivates your child. Two primary things kids want are *time* (to do things they enjoy) and *freedom* (to choose how they will spend that time). Using age and maturity as a factor, strong motivators can include having access to electronic devices, spending time with friends, using the car, participating in unchaperoned events and the opportunity to earn money.

Teach your children the concept of earning their free time. Like a bank account in which deposits are made, rewards can directly correlate to completed responsibilities. For instance:

- Homework done: 30 minutes earned.
- Bedroom clean: 20 minutes.
- Dishwasher unloaded: 10 minutes.

There are no shortcuts to intentionally raising great children. There are, however, time-tested principles you can instill in your child—and the principle of cause and effect is a major one! Shielding your children from the consequences of their actions only sets them up for difficult times later. Teaching responsibility and accountability will give *you* the confidence to know your child is ready to stand on his or her own two feet when the time comes.

Being a Professional

These days many women work outside the home, married or not. It's just a reality of life that most households require (or prefer) two incomes. Many women also find a job or career very satisfying and stimulating. If you are also a wife and mom, it gets much more challenging to achieve balance.

Oftentimes we struggle to not let work spill over to our home life, and vice versa. By its very nature a job often takes up the bulk of our day, and often our energy. When we come home our family may feel like they're getting what's *left over*, after we've given our job our best.

Intentionality becomes an even greater necessity. How do you prioritize your marriage and children and demonstrate to them that they are more important, even though you have fewer hours to give them? How do you battle exhaustion so that you can be emotionally and mentally present at home, not just physically? Are you trying to do everything or are you delegating? Are you and your husband working together as team players, or not?

Being a *professional* applies to all your roles, not just your place of employment. A professional woman embodies characteristics that go beyond just dressing a certain way. She is competent yet humble. She is responsible and manages herself (and others) well. She regulates her emotions, especially under stress, and doesn't allow a difficult person or situation to impact or ruin her day. She knows when she needs help and asks for it. And above all, she has integrity. She never compromises who she is, or what she believes in. As a result, she is respected, trusted, and even loved, by those who rely on her (Proverbs 31:10–31).

That's a tall order! None of us live this perfectly of course. But it's certainly an ideal to strive towards.

Intentional Communication

Being intentional means learning to communicate effectively. What happens though, when there's a breakdown in communication?

Alison is 24. She just recently married her boyfriend of two years, and though they're very happy now, they struggled initially.

"I was bullied severely at school as a kid. And then, at home, I was told not to be so sensitive, to not be a wimp," she shared with me. She grew up in an environment where everyone always seemed angry. Between home and school, it felt easier to put up a wall around people. It didn't help that her first boyfriend was emotionally inaccessible. "I realize now that I adopted some of his private, reserved nature," she told me.

When she met Greg, she struggled to open up to him early on. For several months their relationship was long distance, and they lived in significantly different time zones, which didn't help. Distractions and other people were taking up more of her time and it was hard to be fully present with him when they did talk.

"It felt overwhelming. The distractions were killing my social battery, but I wasn't sharing that with him," she admits now.

Greg finally conveyed to her his frustrations, but it was difficult for her to change. "I didn't see it as a big problem at first. Instead I felt attacked by him for not talking about how I was feeling."

She began to feel like the depth and substance of their relationship was gone. They began making assumptions about each other, each other's needs and their communication styles.

Over time, Alison realized that she'd been trying to protect herself because she didn't want to come across as desperate or vulnerable. She knew that if she didn't change it would ruin them. Once she acknowledged this she was able to work on being more intentional about what she wanted and needed to share with Greg. She learned to not hold things in, which led to several discussions that weren't always easy, but ultimately led to a deeper bond between them.

That's what intentional communication is all about.

When you know what you really want, and what God wants for you, you still need to be able to talk about that with others, because you *need* them. You can't do it alone.

How you communicate your needs is essential. Have you considered your audience? How might he or she best hear you? Do you think about the way you ask, before asking? Can you explain yourself clearly and confidently? Are you asking for permission or are you outlining the pros and cons of a situation in a logical way?

When you ask for permission, you are giving someone else the authority to tell you "no." And perhaps they do have that authority, but there's a way to ask that leads to much greater success than just saying "Would it be okay if I…?" Don't afraid to be vulnerable or have your wishes rejected. That will happen occasionally, because we don't always get what we want, nor should we.

What about the other person(s) affected by your intentions? Have you considered their needs? Their perspective?

Communication is far more than words. Your tone and facial expression, the inflection of your words, your body posture—these convey a message as well. It's okay, even necessary, to take a stand on things that matter to you. Discuss them in a way that preserves peace, unity, and harmony. If you try to get your way through manipulation or underhandedness it will undermine both your efforts and the relationship. Instead, be honest and clear about what you want and why you want it.

It's one thing to know all these things. It's another matter to apply them in your own life, or if you do try to apply them, to be met with silence or have your motives questioned. Communication is a two-way process. You can resolve to be more intentional in your relationships and in the way you communicate, but sometimes it doesn't work.

The Heart of the Matter

Everything about Jordan was unexpected, in the best possible ways. Though we'd gone through some brief training before leaving home, it didn't prepare us fully. We knew it would be safe, relatively speaking. We'd been told the people were friendly. We had a basic idea of where we'd be living and working. The rest we learned by being there.

Those first initial days were packed with discoveries. An administrator from the school I would be working at immediately made himself available to us and took our small group of five to Carrefour, the local equivalent of Wal Mart. We set up our phones, bank accounts, unpacked and took the opportunity to rent a car and explore part of the country before the semester started.

Our work week was Sunday through Thursday. Each day started early. My school bus typically picked me up anywhere between 7:15 and 7:30 a.m. My husband's school was much further away so his bus came around 6:30 a.m.

Afternoons were filled with various things like grocery shopping, exercise, and dinner preparations. We didn't have a car so we either walked or took an Uber most places.

We quickly settled into a routine, and I found myself very content at work. I'd been placed in an office to assist the director of co-curricular activities for students in 11th and 12th grade. I enjoyed it a lot. I felt valued and useful and I quickly came to know the students by name as they popped in and out of our office each day for various reasons.

It had been a long time since I'd worked for someone else and I'd forgotten the camaraderie that comes with being part of a team. I found myself looking forward to going to work each day. Coming home was a different matter.

Though we were in a very different country and culture, my husband and I hadn't changed anything about our communication at home. We weren't talking, except about day-to-day matters. We stayed busy. We shopped together, ran other errands, and explored the country as time and money permitted. Any attempts I made to discuss life beyond Jordan didn't go far.

At this point, our home had sold and our ranch was finally under contract. We were getting close to having the financial means to put a down payment on a new home once we returned to Texas. Again, any conversation about where we would live and what we would do never happened.

We weren't fighting. We had, however, taken on roles in our relationship that were contrary to a biblically-based, healthy marriage. As I found myself happier at work than at home, I began to question things. Until finally, one evening I determined to communicate to my husband how I really felt.

WORKBOOK

Chapter Ten Questions

Question: How happy are you? What makes you happy? What keeps you from being happier?

_____
_____
_____
_____
_____
_____
_____
_____
_____

Question: How are you being intentional in your current roles? As a single, a wife, a mom, or a professional?

Question: How can you make your communication with God and others more intentional?

Action: Determine what time of day you will schedule your time with God and with yourself. What do you want to discuss or learn in your time with God, the next time you meet? What do you want to accomplish during your time with yourself? What tools will you want to bring with you to your appointments?

Chapter Ten Notes

CHAPTER ELEVEN

Forgiveness

I want to share one last thing as you get ready to start down your new path. You need to forgive, and you need to ask for God's forgiveness. Then, you need to move forward.

You don't get to be the age you are without some tragedy and trauma. People have hurt you. You've hurt yourself, and others. If you want to take the path less traveled, the divinely guided path, you need to acknowledge those hurts and then let them go.

That means you can't let them hold any power over you anymore. Holding on to hurt, anger, and grudges about real or imagined offenses is like carrying around a container of toxic waste that's eating away at you. Choosing to not forgive destroys you from the inside out.

The Rest of the Story

That night in Jordan when I talked with my husband, I was the most direct I'd ever been. Perhaps I was too direct. That conversation led to a separation, which essentially meant separate bedrooms under the same roof.

The next few months were an emotional hell for both

of us, yet we still couldn't talk in any kind of productive way. I wanted us to get professional help but there was nowhere to go in Jordan. In the meantime, I'd been offered a permanent position with the school in Amman and my husband and I had agreed, prior to "the talk," to return for a second year.

After the separation, my husband changed his mind about returning to Jordan, but I was still hopeful about coming back. I wanted to find a way to return home for the summer, where perhaps we could find a counselor who would continue to work with me virtually when I returned to Jordan in the fall, while my husband stayed in the U.S. Maybe we could find a way, for the first time, to work through our conflicts to find resolution.

That was not to be. Our stay in Jordan ended abruptly when my husband's health suddenly deteriorated, and he had to go home. Three weeks later I returned to the U.S. for a previously scheduled commitment. But right before I left, I was informed by the board of our international program that instead of returning to Jordan as scheduled, I would not be finishing the year.

With only two days' notice to my job I packed up everything, said my goodbyes, and left the country.

I lived with my sister and her family for the next six months while I waited and wondered whether or not there would be any attempt at reconciliation with my husband. Our last face-to-face contact had been the morning before he flew home. From that point forward he'd been unwilling to talk with me and would only text me if he needed information.

It was a confusing time, but I stayed busy. Confusing, because I didn't know what the future looked like and because so much that I found bewildering had happened so quickly. It was an emotionally challenging time too. My thoughts and feelings were roller coasting up and down at high speeds and all I could do was hang on tightly.

When I first got back, I had a decision to make. Would I give up my professional dreams and apply for a nine-to-five job, or not? It wasn't a tough decision, even though the idea of starting my business from the ground up again was daunting. I'd started a business before and I'd sustained it, though minimally, through all the moves and changes. This time, however, I wanted to hire people who had marketing skills that I didn't have.

Within a month of returning from the Middle East I'd hired a website designer and social media expert and scheduled a photo shoot for the website. I signed a lease on an office and began working with my website designer and editor to turn a course I'd written for women into a polished, professional product. I began writing blogs in anticipation of the website going live and I looked for a part-time counseling job on the side.

Focusing on things that I could be intentional about got me through those challenging months. With the help of my own therapist I was reminded that there were so many things I didn't have control over: people's opinions, my husband's unwillingness to talk, even my own emotions often felt like a runaway train. I could change the latter. So, I did.

Even therapists are not immune to faulty thinking! Therapy gave me the outside perspective I needed. It challenged me to stop feeling sorry for myself and instead, start asking some tough questions.

> *What was my contribution to our marital problems?*
>
> *Why did I behave that way?*
>
> *Why do I think this way?*
>
> *Where do my underlying beliefs about certain*

things come from?"

Even as I did the work I was asked to do, as time went by it became clear that my husband and I would not be reconciling. Though I had many questions with no answers, I was also gaining clarity about my marriage that only time and distance from each other could give me.

That clarity helped me to understand some of the challenges we'd faced our entire marriage, in a different light. With that clarity I began to gain a different perspective, one that helped me to accept things and move forward.

And yes, to forgive.

Principles of Forgiveness

No one grows up in a perfect home or has the perfect relationship. No one does the best he or she can all the time. We all end up *broken* at some point, and we give what we can out of our brokenness. That's why loving others requires so much patience. God's ideal is that we treat people the way we want to be treated (Matthew 7:12). If you want people to be forgiving of your imperfections, you must learn to do the same for them. However, not all broken things can be fixed in this lifetime. Sometimes we just have to accept that and move forward. Forgive, and ask for forgiveness.

We can have a hard time with this, however, often because we don't properly understand forgiveness.

For example, you might struggle with certain beliefs:

- You might believe that forgiveness means that what happened was *okay*. It wasn't.

- You might think you're letting the other

person get away with something or that you're letting them off the hook. You're not.

- You may think forgiveness means restoring the relationship, even if what that other person did is still happening. It doesn't. You can forgive and yet not reconcile with someone.

What Is Forgiveness?

It's a spiritual gift from God. The concept of forgiveness is a biblical one. God gives us forgiveness when we come to Him, acknowledge our sins and repent of them (Acts 3:19). It can be challenging to believe that God—who is omnipotent, all-knowing, and all-powerful—loves you enough to forgive your sins *and* removes them from you (Psalm 103:12). He does, and so must we.

It's a requirement. God also requires us to forgive others as He forgives us (Matthew 6:14–15). It's impossible to be divinely intentional without doing so. Forgiveness is like a salve that soothes, cools and heals wounds caused by others. While you will likely never forget as God does—because you are, after all, human—forgiveness allows you to move forward instead of getting bogged down on that familiar path of resentments, grudges, and broken promises.

It's an act of love. Children make lots of mistakes growing up, yet parents forgive them. Why? Love. If we didn't love our children, we would have a hard time raising them. We would struggle with their concrete thinking, their self-centeredness and their willful natures.

Have you ever considered that it's the same for God? His ways and thoughts are so different from ours (Isaiah 55:9). While He wants us to strive to think and behave like Him, He created us, so He's fully aware of our human limitations. In fact, He knows us better than we know ourselves. He loves us unconditionally, and He shows us incredible compassion and mercy, over and over, despite our shortcomings.

There's a parable in the Bible that really illustrates this (Matthew 18:21–35). It's about a man who begs for forgiveness of a large debt he's owed, but then turns around and shows no mercy to someone who owes him a pittance.

How can we ask for God to be patient and understanding with us, but deal harshly with others? How can we assume that we know others' motives yet walk around feeling misunderstood and misrepresented? How can we ask for God's forgiveness but nurture seeds of anger until they bloom into full blown hatred?

Sometimes we don't believe God has really forgiven us. We doubt His love. We feel we've made too many mistakes or sinned too much. We forget that we are all sinners. None of us is *deserving* of God's forgiveness, or His love. He gives us His love freely, because of who He is, not who we are.

Negative thoughts about how worthless and undeserving you are, are unproductive. That kind of negative self-talk impacts your daily decision-making. Intentional living isn't about beating yourself up. It's about recognizing that sometimes you sabotage yourself with your thoughts and behaviors, and the way you interact with other people. The quicker you realize that, the quicker you can focus on making changes and getting back on track.

Some people, however, think it's too late for them.

It's never too late.

I talk to God all the time, even knowing there are times when He is disappointed in the things I do. I still feel loved.

That doesn't mean there aren't consequences for my actions. There are. It doesn't change how He feels about me. I still believe in and accept His forgiveness. These days you hear a lot about needing to "forgive yourself." I disagree. It's God's forgiveness that cleanses us of sins, not our own. If God says you are forgiven when you go to Him and repent, then you are. Don't throw that forgiveness back in His face by refusing its transformative power.

It's an opportunity for growth. There is a freedom that comes from forgiving. When you forgive others, you remove the emotional power they hold over you.

It's not easy. You don't just say the words "I forgive," and then—poof!—instantaneous forgiveness granted. It's an arduous, painful process that involves a whole lot of soul-searching. But it's important to remember that forgiveness isn't for the other person. Forgiveness is for you.

Why?

Because the alternative is damaging. Only when you forgive can you truly heal and move forward. It's hard to be proactive if you're emotionally stuck.

You can't truly forgive someone without it changing you, for the better. That doesn't mean, however, that you won't still hurt. Forgiving others doesn't wipe away your pain. It can be extremely difficult to forgive someone who has failed to apologize. Sometimes it's not possible to talk with someone about the situation; he or she may not allow it, or you know it will do more harm than good. You can, however, always talk to God about it and tell Him everything. He will listen and understand. More importantly, His Holy Spirit will comfort and guide you in *how* to forgive and let go, over time. Releasing the pain through tools like journaling, exercise, even therapy, can be useful as well. You will know when you have made progress when you can say, "I understand that's who you are. I don't like that part about you, but I accept it. I am ready to stop letting it negatively affect me."

It's not the same as reconciliation. Reconciliation requires change. To be reconciled to God you have to repent, ask for forgiveness, and then strive to change your life.

The same is true with your other relationships. The act of forgiveness does not obligate people to let you into their life again, or vice versa. People who've hurt you have to stop hurting you. They have to acknowledge the hurt, apologize for it, and then strive to never hurt you again. They have to accept the consequences of that hurt; the damage it's created, instead of insisting that an apology should be enough for things to return to "normal."

If those things don't happen, you may choose to not interact with them in the same way ever again, or at all, even if you've forgiven their past behavior. This choice shouldn't be a punishment but a protection for you, against further hurt. Remember, you too have (or will) hurt someone equally as bad, and someday you will want forgiveness from that person. You may hope to be part of that person's life again. Whatever standard you hold others too, know that you too will be held to that same standard (Matthew 7:2).

And So It Is

I've been divorced for a while now. I'm not going to say that it's all been easy, because that would be untrue. Nor will I say that it was all my husband's fault because that would be foolish and also untrue. Could things have turned out differently?

Yes, but they didn't.

If I've learned anything through this, I've learned that I cannot change others, no matter how much I may want to. I can only change myself.

I can forgive my husband for the hurt and damage he caused me, and I can hope that he's done the same. I can ask God's forgiveness for my role in the dissolution of our marriage. I can believe that God has forgiven me, and even more importantly, has forgotten my sins completely.

God expects me to move forward, to not get bogged down on the familiar path. He wants me to look to Him for guidance and direction, trust the path He's set before me, *the path less traveled*. He doesn't promise it will be easy or obstacle-free. He does say He will be with me every step of the way, as long as I keep my eyes on Him and let Him direct my steps. So, with intention, off I go.

I hope to see you there! More importantly, God wants you there. Your life will be better for it—not easier, but better. It doesn't matter what you've gone through or what you're struggling with right now. God knows. He cares. He wants more for you than you have right now. Believe that, seek it wholeheartedly and you will find it.

> "For I am persuaded that neither death nor life, nor angels nor principalities nor powers, nor things present nor things to come, nor height nor depth, nor any other created thing, shall be able to separate us from the love of God which is in Christ Jesus our Lord."
> —***Romans 8:38–39***

WORKBOOK

Chapter Eleven Questions

Question: Describe a time when you have experienced or witnessed the power of forgiveness in a seemingly impossible situation. How can working through the process of forgiveness lead to personal growth and freedom?

_____
_____
_____
_____
_____
_____
_____
_____
_____

Question: Have you accepted God's forgiveness for you,

or do you hold onto guilt and regret over things from the past? How can you fully realize God's forgiveness for you? Does God's forgiveness motivate you to forgive others?

_____
_____
_____
_____
_____
_____
_____
_____
_____
_____

Action: If you are facing a situation that requires exceptional forgiveness, consider seeing a counselor or therapist or talking to a pastor or Christian mentor. They can help you work through the right steps to take and what your relationship with the offender should look like going forward.

Chapter Eleven Notes

CONCLUSION

Seeking an Abundant Life

So many women are drifting through life because they have not learned how to want what God wants for them; an intentional life filled with divinely-led purpose (John 10:10). This doesn't happen automatically.

With our relationship with God as our foundation, we can step into truly intentional living. Intentional living is living that is based on dreams that align with our values. It's about planning, commitment, prioritizing, self-care, and a heart inclined toward forgiveness. Above all, intentional living is about relationships, beginning with our relationship with our heavenly Father, and continuing to every other relationship in our lives.

As we align ourselves with God's plan and perspective, we find a self-worth not dependent on anything or anyone else—one that will sustain us in pursuing our hopes and dreams.

You are a beautiful woman created in God's image, and He has a wonderful plan, with you—specifically—in mind. Embrace your quality time with Him, and with yourself, using the tools provided, and unearth your potential as a woman living out God's purpose for your life.

To learn more about how to do this, check out the

course I've created, A Christian Woman's Guide to Intentional Living, at www.bydivinedesignforwomen.com.

Or reach out to me and we'll craft an intentional living plan for you together!

REFERENCES

Notes

1. Johnson, Matthew D. *Great Myths of Intimate Relationships: Dating, Sex, and Marriage.* Wiley-Blackwell, 2016.

2. The Duke of Edinburgh's International Award is a non-competitive, internationally recognized program designed to encourage personal challenge and development. (See: "What Is the Award?" The Duke of Edinburgh's International Award. https://www.dukeofed.org/what-is-the-award.)

3. Haughey, Duncan. "A Brief History of Smart Goals." Project Smart. 2014. https://www.projectsmart.co.uk/brief-history-of-smart-goals.php.

4. Duhigg, Charles. *The Power of Habit: Why We Do What We Do in Life and Business.* Random House Publishing Group, 2012.

5. Project Meditation. "Writing Goals Down Versus Just Thinking About Them." 2018. https://www.project-meditation.org/writing-goals/.

6. LeVan, Angie. "Seeing Is Believing: The Power of Visualization." Psychology Today. December 3, 2009. https://www.psychologytoday.com/us/blog/flourish/200912/seeing-is-believing-the-power-visualization.

7. Antanaityte, Neringa. "Mind Matters: How to Effortlessly Have More Positive Thoughts." TLEX Institute. https://tlexinstitute.com/how-to-effortlessly-have-more-positive-thoughts/.

About the Author

Hi, I'm Debbie Caudle, Licensed Mental Health Therapist for over 25 years and lover of all things international. My path less traveled has taken me to many countries and I have built relationships with women all over the globe—professionally and personally.

I love helping others on their journey of self-improvement, and I'm devoted to it in every aspect of my own health. My journey is not over, so as long as I'm still learning, I will continue to pass my knowledge on to others. That's part of my purpose, and I'll strive to fulfill it for as long as God allows.

About Speak It To Book

Speak It to Book, the premier ghostwriting agency and publisher for faith-filled thought leaders, is revolutionizing how books are created and used.

We are a team of world-changing people who are passionate about making your great ideas famous.

Imagine:

- What if you had a way to beat writer's block, overcome your busy schedule, and get all of those ideas out of your head?
- What if you could partner with a team to crush lack of motivation and productivity so you can get your

story in front of the people who need it most?

- What if you took that next step into significance and influence, using your book to launch your platform?
- What if you could write your book with a team of professionals from start to finish?

Your ideas are meant for a wider audience. Visit www.speakittobook.com to schedule a call with our team of Jesus-loving publishing professionals today.

www.ingramcontent.com/pod-product-compliance
Lightning Source LLC
Chambersburg PA
CBHW070849050426
42453CB00012B/2099